Resource Manual
for

CIVIL
LITIGATION
FOR
PARALEGALS

ELIZABETH C. RICHARDSON, J.D.
ADJUNCT FACULTY
CENTRAL PIEDMONT COMMUNITY COLLEGE

MILTON C. REGAN, JR., J.D.
ASSOCIATE PROFESSOR
GEORGETOWN UNIVERSITY LAW CENTER

LQ40AD
PUBLISHED BY
SOUTH-WESTERN PUBLISHING CO.
CINCINNATI, OH   DALLAS, TX   LIVERMORE, CA

3 4 5 6 7 8 9 0 MT 0 9 8 7 6 5 4 3
Printed in the United States of America

PREFACE

The student Resource Manual is an integral tool for the paralegal student to gain an understanding of civil litigation. The student Resource Manual enables students to review every chapter in *Civil Litigation for Paralegals* in detail.

For each chapter there are three sections to aid students in their review of all the important concepts in the textbook. The first section is the Summary. The Summary is a narrative review of the important rules and concepts covered in each chapter.

The second section is entitled Study Questions. The Study Questions are a series of short discussion questions that require students to explain the important rules and procedures in each chapter. The Study Questions also require students to explain important litigation terms introduced in each chapter.

The third section is entitled Test Your Knowledge. The Test Your Knowledge section contains objective study questions, including multiple choice, true/false, and completion exercises. This serves as a further review of the important terms and rules in each chapter.

At the end of the exercises for each chapter are the answers both for the Study Questions and the Test Your Knowledge section. Thus students are able to review on their own. Teachers who prefer review in the classroom can have students remove the pages with test questions and complete them in class.

Students who read the Summary and complete the Study Questions and Test Your Knowledge questions for each chapter should have an in-depth understanding of the important terms, rules, and concepts covered in each chapter. The student Resource Manual for *Civil Litigation for Paralegals* will enhance paralegal students' knowledge of civil litigation and prepare them to be effective members of the attorney/paralegal team.

Elizabeth C. Richardson
Milton C. Regan, Jr.

CONTENTS

1 INTRODUCTION TO CIVIL LITIGATION AND THE LAW OFFICE

SUMMARY

Chapter 1 gives an overview of the litigation process and an introduction to working in a law office, including office procedures important for litigation paralegals. The first important concept is the order in which a lawsuit progresses. First, the incident that necessitates a lawsuit occurs. This is called the cause of action. After the initial client conference, in which the basic facts are received from the client, the attorney/paralegal team conducts further investigation, such as interviewing potential witnesses and checking public records. Next, the complaint and summons are drafted and served on the defendant. The defendant then does some investigation and files an answer and/or other response, such as a motion to dismiss. The litigation then enters the discovery phase, in which all parties conduct formal investigation of the facts through interrogatories, depositions, and other discovery methods. After some discovery, the parties can usually determine whether they may be entitled to judgment without trial through the methods of judgment on the pleadings or summary judgment. Note that earlier in the litigation process, if the defendant failed to respond to the complaint in a timely manner, the plaintiff could seek a default judgment.

The parties may file a wide range of other pretrial motions, such as motions to amend pleadings or motions to compel a response to a discovery request. By this point, the parties may explore settlement possibilities. Frequently settlement is reached at the final pretrial conference, where the attorneys for each party meet with the presiding judge to define and narrow the issues, determine witnesses and exhibits, and perhaps have the judge rule on some pretrial motions such as those concerning the admissibility of certain evidence.

Preparation for the actual trial includes issuing subpoenas for witnesses to appear, copying and organizing exhibits, and a host of other tasks. After a verdict is entered, if there is no appeal, the prevailing party takes the necessary steps to enforce the judgment. If an appeal is entered, the record on appeal must be prepared, together with an appellate brief.

The second major concept in this chapter has to do with the rules that govern civil procedure to ensure an orderly litigation process in a busy court system.

If you are litigating in federal court, the Federal Rules of Civil Procedure must be followed. In federal court you must also follow the local court rules, which address some of the more ministerial concerns such as how many copies of a document to file and the size of paper, as well as more substantive matters such as how many days are allowed for a response to a motion before the motion is deemed unopposed and the court's method for scheduling arguments on motions.

In state court, you must follow that state's rules of civil procedure. These rules will probably mirror the federal rules to some extent but can differ in such important areas as the amount of time allowed to file an answer to a complaint. State courts may have local rules of court that address the same matters discussed in federal local rules. There may be a further set of local rules for that particular state judicial district. When in doubt about any rules, confer with your supervising attorney or call the office of the clerk of court.

Also important are the federal and state rules of evidence, which govern whether evidence is admissible. Finally, it is always important to bear in mind the rules of professional responsibility that govern the conduct of attorneys. Although paralegals cannot be disciplined directly for conduct in violation of the rules of professional responsibility, the attorneys for whom they work can be disciplined for the paralegals' conduct.

The third important concept in Chapter 1 is the types of lawsuits in which paralegals may be involved. Lawsuits span a wide range of subject matters. One common type of suit is the tort, which is initiated when the negligent conduct of one person has caused bodily injury and/or property damage to another. Another object of frequent litigation is a contract, when one party to an agreement fails to fulfill its terms. A wide range of matters related to corporations may be litigated, from contract disputes to employment disputes. Disagreements also arise over property, both real property (land) and personal property (other types of possession, such as jewelry or cars). Civil rights litigation may involve major constitutional questions and alleged violations of federal and state statutes. An example is the Chattooga case, which involves Title VII of the Civil Rights Act. Title VII lawsuits are preceded by administrative proceedings in which the Equal Employment Opportunity Commission (EEOC) attempts to fashion a conciliation without a trial. The process of completing all administrative procedures and appeals before filing a lawsuit is known as exhaustion of administrative remedies. This is frequently a prerequisite to filing an action in court when an administrative agency is involved.

The next major area concerns the remedies available through litigation. Plaintiffs frequently ask for money damages—that is, monetary compensation for the injuries and losses suffered. A plaintiff may seek an equitable remedy when facing a loss for which there can be no monetary compensation. An example is an injunction, which is a court order to refrain from an act.

It is important to understand the basic setup and office procedures of a law firm. There are generally two types of lawyers in a firm. First are the partners, who own the firm, derive compensation based on the firm's profits, and make management decisions. Second are associates, who are usually the more recently hired lawyers and receive a set salary. Some law firms employ law clerks, law students who are not licensed and who usually perform research and writing duties. Providing an important staff function are the paralegals, who possess legal skills and work under the direct supervision of attorneys. Linking these professionals you will find a variety of support personnel, including legal secretaries, word processors, receptionists, and file clerks; the number and exact positions will depend in part on the size of the firm.

The litigation atmosphere is different from that of other types of law. The schedule of litigators is controlled more by the courts than by the lawyers themselves. An attorney will litigate several cases simultaneously and may have several court appearances in one week, as well as ongoing discovery procedures and pleadings that are due. Paralegals are essential in helping the litigator to meet all deadlines and avoid overlooking anything. Litigators come in all personality types, and you must adjust to the personalities of your coworkers and remember that the litigation atmosphere can be tense when time pressures abound.

Paralegals have many important law office procedures to learn for their particular firms. Some of the most important involve timekeeping and billing. There are two common types of fee agreements. One is the hourly rate, in which the client agrees to an amount per hour for the billable time devoted to the case. The other major type of fee agreement is the contingent fee, in which the law firm receives a certain percentage of the award received by the plaintiff, often one-third. In addition, clients are generally billed for disbursements such as postage, xerox copies, and travel. Thus it is apparent that you must keep careful records of the disbursements and of your time and tasks performed. There are a variety of methods for keeping time records. Many firms have each attorney and paralegal keep a written record of the time spent and tasks performed, and this information is entered into the computer billing system at the end of each day, week, or month. From this information, the client is sent a monthly bill. Time is usually recorded by tenths of an hour, so if you spent an hour and 18 minutes drafting a complaint, this would be 1.30 hours.

Because billable hours is such a crucial factor, paralegals must employ time management techniques such as filling out time slips promptly, keeping a list of tasks to be performed and consulting it each morning, reviewing files regularly using a tickler system to schedule a manageable number of files per day, and performing the most difficult tasks first thing in the morning. In addition, paralegals should meet regularly with the attorneys on their team to discuss cases.

One of the most crucial tasks assigned to paralegals is docket control, which is keeping track of the deadlines for filing pleadings and memoranda of law, completing discovery, and all the many deadlines that litigation entails. A variety of docket control systems exist, and you can use multiple systems so that you have a backup. Computerized docket systems have become common and can produce printouts of upcoming deadlines. Computerized systems can also flash deadline warnings on your word processor screen every morning. A manual system is the tickler form, where you fill out the name and file number of the case, together with the action to be taken, the deadline, and the reminder dates you desire.

The forms are given to a person who is responsible for distributing the reminder slips to you on the designated days. Many attorneys and paralegals enter deadlines on calendars, but with this method you must review the upcoming weeks carefully and enter reminders as well as the actual deadlines.

In order to keep apprised of all impending deadlines, paralegals must review all incoming mail, monitor court calendars, and check the docket sheets in the files in the office of the clerk of court. Litigation paralegals should keep in each file a pleadings record to note the pleadings filed and when responses are due.

In addition to deadlines for filing and responding to pleadings, other deadlines include statutes of limitations, which govern the time allowed for commencement of a lawsuit after a cause of action arises. You must consult the applicable federal or state statute, and this is one of the first tasks you address when a new client comes in. Deadlines are also imposed in the discovery process. For example, if a timely response to requests for admissions is not made, important matters may be deemed admitted. Motions must also be filed within certain limitations, as must responses to motions. Court appearances for hearings or trial are obviously important dates to enter into the docket control system. Even after the trial, time limitations apply to entering notice of appeal and submitting the record on appeal and filing certain post-trial motions.

Another very important function of paralegals is to maintain regular communications with clients by telephone, meetings, and letters. Informing clients of deadlines for submitting information and following up are very important duties. When communicating orally, you will often dictate a memorandum to the file to record the substance of your conversation. Paralegals must be cautious not to render legal advice. Instead, relay the facts and questions to the attorney, and let the attorney call the client to render the advice. If the attorney is tied up in trial, get the legal advice in writing and relay it to the client, emphasizing that it constitutes the attorney's opinion, not yours.

Finally, Chapter 1 addresses the litigation tasks commonly assigned to paralegals. Paralegals are essential to successful litigation, as can be seen by the vast array of duties they perform. Review the tasks outlined in Chapter 1, which are arranged according to the stage of litigation at which the task is generally performed. You will see that you have much to look forward to.

Chapter 1   Introduction to Civil Litigation and the Law Office

STUDY QUESTIONS

1. Define the term civil litigation.

   lawsuits involving only noncriminal matters

2. Explain what a cause of action is and what constitutes the cause of action in the Wesser case.

   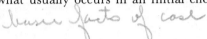
   event, state of facts that gives rise to a claim burn out electrical blanket

3. Describe what usually occurs in an initial client conference.

   basic facts of case

4. How are defendants informed that they have been sued, and what happens if they do not respond after being informed?

   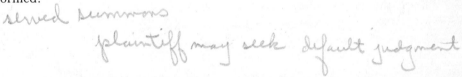
   served summons
   plaintiff may seek default judgment

5. Explain what discovery is and discuss two major discovery devices.

   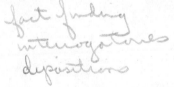
   fact finding
   interrogatories
   depositions

6. What usually takes place at a pretrial conference?

7. What steps follow the entry of judgment?

8. Describe the rules that govern civil litigation in federal and state court.

9. What is the purpose of the preceding rules?

10. Define the terms *torts* and *product liability*.

11. Explain the meaning of breach of contract and give an example.

12. Explain the difference between money damages and equitable remedies.

13. Explain the term *court calendar*.

14. Explain the difference between a fee agreement for an hourly rate and a contingent fee.

15. Explain the entries paralegals should make on their time slips.

16. List some time management techniques to help paralegals use their time at the office efficiently.

17. Describe three docket control systems.

18. Discuss the common sources for determining deadlines to enter in the docket control system.

19. What are some of the most important deadlines to be entered in the docket control system?

20. Why are regular communications with clients essential?

21. Name some of the tasks paralegals may perform prior to commencement of the lawsuit.

TEST YOUR KNOWLEDGE

COMPLETION

From the list of key terms below, select the term that best completes each sentence.

court calendar   pleadings
deposition   pleadings record
discovery   product liability
equitable remedy   service of process
exhaustion of administrative remedies   summons

1. When a lawsuit involves an administrative agency, and regulations require that certain steps be taken through the agency before commencement of a lawsuit, this is known as _____ _____ .

2. Delivery of the summons and complaint to a defendant in accordance with FRCivP 4 is called _____ .

3. The schedule of trials and hearings for a given day or week is called a docket or _____ .

4. A type of litigation resulting from damages caused by an allegedly defective product such as an electric blanket is called _____ .

5. The document delivered to defendants to inform them that a lawsuit has been filed against them is called a _____ .

6. The formal documents in which parties allege their claims and defenses are called _____ _____ .

7. The formal process through which parties gain information from each other during litigation is called _____ .

8. An _____ remedy is requested when money damages cannot compensate a party; one example is an injunction.

9. A _____ is part of the docket control system and is kept in a conspicuous place in the office file.

10. The discovery device where an attorney orally examines a witness is a _____ .

TRUE/FALSE

1. (T) F   A statute of limitations defines the time within which a lawsuit must be commenced.

2. (T) F   Specific performance is an equitable remedy in which the court orders a party to perform the terms of a contract.

3. T (F)   The owners and managers of a law firm are called associates.

4. T **F** When a lawyer's fee is based on the amount the plaintiff recovers, this is known as an hourly rate.

5. **T** F To keep track of pleadings, paralegals should check the file in the clerk of court's office.

6. T **F** Discovery deadlines are usually not enforced and need not be placed in the docket control system.

7. T **F** State rules of civil procedure are identical to the Federal Rules of Civil Procedure.

8. T **F** The Federal Rules of Civil Procedure cover pretrial matters only.

9. **T** F Local court rules may impose deadlines to be entered in the docket control system.

10. T **F** When a defendant fails to respond to a complaint, the plaintiff should seek summary judgment.

11. **T** F The event that gives rise to a claim for which a plaintiff seeks relief from the court is called a cause of action.

12. T **F** It is unethical to bill clients for disbursement such as postage and copies.

13. T **F** After a verdict is entered, a party may file a notice of appeal within any reasonable time.

14. T **F** The admissibility of evidence is governed primarily by local court rules.

15. T **F** It is unethical for paralegals to assist with witness preparation.

Chapter 1   Introduction to Civil Litigation and the Law Office

ANSWERS TO STUDY QUESTIONS

1. Civil litigation is the process of carrying on a lawsuit. A plaintiff files a lawsuit to seek a remedy from a court. Civil litigation involves only noncriminal actions.

2. A cause of action is the event that causes the damages for which a plaintiff seeks relief from a court. The cause of action in the Wesser case is the fire, allegedly caused by a defective electric blanket, which injured Mr. Wesser and damaged his house.

3. The lawyer obtains the basic facts from the potential client and assesses whether the client has a cause of action. The lawyer explains in general how the lawsuit will proceed. If the client decides to hire the lawyer, they enter a fee agreement.

4. The plaintiff files a complaint, stating allegations against the defendants. The complaint and summons, which is a form stating that a person has been sued and has a certain amount of time to respond, are delivered to the defendants. This delivery is called service of process. The defendants should respond within the allotted time by filing an answer and/or motions to dismiss. If the defendants do not respond, it is assumed that they do not contest the facts alleged in the complaint, and default judgment may be entered against them.

5. After the initial pleadings are filed, the parties begin the discovery process, which is the formal process through which the parties obtain information about the lawsuit from each other. One discovery device is the deposition, where an attorney asks questions to a person under oath, and the answers are recorded by a court reporter. Interrogatories are another major discovery device. These are written questions sent to the opposing parties, who must submit written answers that they swear to be true.

6. The attorneys and the presiding judge meet to try to narrow the issues and facts in dispute. They also discuss the exhibits and witnesses to be presented at trial, and the judge may rule on some motions regarding admissibility of evidence. Finally, they try to settle the case; many cases are settled at this stage.

7. If the judgment is not appealed, the prevailing party takes the steps necessary to enforce the judgment—for example, to get the other party to pay the sum ordered. A dissatisfied party may appeal the judgment to an appellate court. If an appeal is filed, a record on appeal must be compiled. The record on appeal includes the pleadings, pertinent parts of the transcript of the trial, and other documents necessary for the appellate court to determine whether the trial court made errors that justify vacating the judgment.

8. In federal court, the Federal Rules of Civil Procedure govern the course of litigation. The FRCivP apply to every step of the litigation, from the types of pleadings allowed to preliminary injunctions to right to jury trial. These rules must be consulted at every step of the litigation process. In state court actions, litigation is governed by that state's rules of civil procedure, which usually are similar to the FRCivP, but may contain important differences such as time allowed to respond to pleadings.

    Federal district courts have their own local rules that supplement the FRCivP and cover such topics as how many copies of documents to file, how to cite cases in a brief, and how to schedule a hearing or pretrial conference. State courts have local rules that govern similar topics.

The Federal Rules of Evidence govern the admissibility of evidence in federal court actions. In state court actions, that state's rules of evidence apply. The state rules of evidence are often similar to the federal, but may contain important differences. The rules of professional responsibility apply to all federal and state litigation.

9. These rules are designed to ensure that litigation proceeds in an orderly manner and that all parties are aware of allegations against them and have the opportunity to respond.

10. Torts are actions in which plaintiffs seek damages for injuries to themselves or their property caused by the wrongful conduct of another person. When the damages are caused by an allegedly defective product, such as Mr. Wesser's electric blanket, the tort litigation is usually referred to as product liability.

11. When two parties enter into a contract, they both agree that one will perform an act in exchange for something from the other. When one party fails to act as promised, the contract has been breached. An example is when a person signs a promissory note agreeing to pay money back and fails to make the payments.

12. Money damages consist of monetary compensation for the loss a person has suffered, such as the damage to Mr. Wesser's house. When a person's claim cannot be compensated by money damages, equitable remedies are necessary. This may take the form of injunctive relief, where a court orders a party to refrain from performing a certain act, such as cutting down a tree. In the Chattooga case, an order that Chattooga Corporation cease discriminatory actions would be injunctive relief. Specific performance is another form of equitable relief. It arises in the context of contract litigation when a court orders a party to perform a certain act, such as sell a piece of property as promised.

13. The court calendar is the schedule of hearings and trials to be heard in a certain court on a particular day or during a particular week. The court calendar is generally published by the administrative office of the court. It is also referred to as a docket or trial list.

14. A fee agreement for an hourly rate means that the client will be billed for the amount of time spent on the case, at an agreed-upon rate per hour. This type of fee agreement usually requires that the client also be responsible for reimbursing the firm for disbursements such as long-distance telephone calls and copies. Under a contingent fee agreement, the attorney receives a certain percentage of the plaintiff's award, frequently one-third.

15. The paralegal should record the client file number, client's name, the paralegal's initials, the code for the type of service rendered, and description of the service. Finally, the paralegal enters the amount of time spent, with periods of less than a full hour recorded by tenths of the hour. There are many methods of keeping track of billable hours, and the information recorded may be either more or less than that described.

16. Paralegals should fill out time slips promptly; keep a list of tasks to be performed, arranged by importance and/or date due; use a tickler system to ensure that files are reviewed regularly; do the most difficult tasks first thing in the morning; meet regularly with the attorneys to discuss cases; and review time sheets to make sure there are sufficient billable hours.

17. Some law firms use a computerized docket control system, which flashes up reminders in the morning and generates lists of deadlines. Some firms use tickler forms, which are forms completed to show the task to be performed and the date it is due. Three or more dates for reminders are entered

on the tickler form, and on those days the paralegal receives a reminder. Deadlines may also be noted on calendars on or near the paralegal's desk, but one must take care to consult the calendars frequently.

18. A readily viewable record of all the proceedings in a case should be kept in the office file. For instance, when a complaint is served, that is noted in the file, together with the date that the response is due. An important part of a file is the pleadings record, to note the information discussed above. Paralegals should also periodically review the file in the clerk of court's office to double-check that all pleadings filed and responses due have been entered in the office file. The clerk's file should also be checked for proof of service of process. Paralegals must also monitor court calendars to note the dates set for hearings and trials. Court calendars come in many forms, from a short schedule mailed to the attorneys involved to periodicals that list multiple court dockets in larger cities.

19. A very important deadline is the statute of limitations, which sets the time within which the plaintiff must file suit. For example, the applicable statute for a breach of contract may require that the action be filed within two years of the breach. If a lawsuit is not filed within the allotted time, the plaintiff is forever barred from filing suit for this particular action.

    The dates by which pleadings must be filed are very important. If responses to pleadings are not filed within the allotted time, the party loses important rights. For example, a default judgment may be entered if a defendant fails to respond to a complaint in a timely manner.

    Discovery deadlines are also important. Parties have only a certain amount of time within which to file answers to interrogatories or finish the depositions they wish to take.

    Deadlines for responding to motions are important for the same reasons deadlines for responding to pleadings are crucial. In many jurisdictions, motions are considered unopposed if no response is filed within a certain time.

    Obviously dates that attorneys must appear in court are important. Deadlines for filing notice of appeal and post-trial motions are also important. Local rules of court may impose additional deadlines.

20. Clients do not like to feel that their case is being neglected. In a protracted lawsuit, there may be no new developments for several weeks, but paralegals need to let the client know that the law firm is taking care of everything. Also, paralegals regularly need to get information from clients to prepare pleadings and respond to discovery requests.

21. Paralegals may attend initial client conferences, perform informal investigation such as checking public records, make preliminary arrangements for expert witnesses, set up files, and obtain additional information from the client.

ANSWERS TO TEST YOUR KNOWLEDGE

COMPLETION

1. exhaustion of administrative remedies
2. service of process
3. court calendar
4. product liability
5. summons

6. pleadings
7. discovery
8. equitable
9. pleadings record
10. deposition

TRUE/FALSE

1. T	6. F	11. T
2. T	7. F	12. F
3. F	8. F	13. F
4. F	9. T	14. F
5. T	10. F	15. F

2 LEGAL ETHICS

SUMMARY

INTRODUCTION

Rules of ethics govern the conduct of attorneys and paralegals. Only attorneys may be disciplined directly for violating ethics rules, but paralegals may cause the attorneys for whom they work to be disciplined if paralegals engage in conduct that violates the ethics rules.

Each state has its own set of ethics rules. Each state regulates the conduct of attorneys licensed to practice law in that state. Although the ultimate power to regulate attorneys is the state supreme court, the state bar is the mechanism for enforcement of the rules. The state bar, working primarily through an ethics committee, can impose sanctions on a lawyer who engages in unethical conduct. The state bar also regulates the admission of lawyers to practice law in that state. Another important function of the state bar is to adopt rules of professional ethics to govern lawyers practicing in the state.

Most states base their ethics rules on those promulgated by the American Bar Association (ABA). In addition to developing model rules of ethics, the ABA undertakes many functions to develop lawyers' knowledge and to improve our system of justice, such as monitoring legislation and sponsoring continuing legal education courses. Membership in the ABA is voluntary, and the ABA accomplishes many tasks through the work of committees.

Many states have a state bar association, with goals similar to those of the ABA. State bar associations sponsor continuing legal education programs and help coordinate *pro bono* legal services.

SOURCES OF ETHICAL GUIDELINES

Most states model their ethics rules after the ABA Model Code of Professional Responsibility (Model Code) or the ABA Model Rules of Professional Conduct (Model Rules). The ABA adopted the Model Rules in 1983, and 35 states have adopted them in some form. Even states that have adopted the Model Rules may retain some portions of the Model Code, so it is important to be familiar with both. Another source for ethical guidance is the ABA's Ethics Opinions. Here, practicing attorneys submit questions concerning ethics, and the ABA publishes an opinion. Some states also publish ethics opinions.

It is important to understand the format of the Model Code. It consists of nine Canons, which are broad statements that express in general terms the standards of conduct expected of lawyers. The canon itself is a short statement and is followed by several ethical considerations (ECs). These are paragraphs that explain in more detail the standards of conduct to which lawyers should aspire. Each canon is also accompanied by disciplinary rules (DRs) that state mandatory rules that lawyers must follow. Violations of disciplinary rules can subject lawyers to disciplinary proceedings.

The format of the Model Rules is different from that of the Model Code. The Model Rules format consists of a rule statement followed by a series of comments that explain the meaning of the rule. Mandatory conduct is set forth in the words ''shall'' or ''shall not,'' whereas nonmandatory rules are expressed as ''may.''

It is imperative that you read in detail your state's rules of ethics. As in the ABA Model Code and Model Rules, the paragraphs beneath the statement of the actual rule are designed to explain the meaning of the rule. Judicial opinions addressing ethical issues are another source for ethical guidance.

EFFECT OF ETHICAL GUIDELINES ON ATTORNEYS AND PARALEGALS

The consequences to an attorney who violates ethical rules can be severe. The severity of the penalty imposed depends on the severity of the violation and surrounding circumstances. Penalties include private reprimand, public reprimand, and suspension from practice for a specific period. The most severe penalty is disbarment, which means that the attorney can no longer practice law in the state.

Attorneys may also be disciplined for conduct not directly related to their representation when the conduct involves dishonesty, fraud, deceit, or misrepresentation. The commission of a crime may subject a lawyer to discipline if the conduct reflects adversely on the attorney's fitness to practice law.

Although paralegals are not directly subject to the penalties that can be imposed on lawyers, they must nevertheless comply with ethics rules. Comment 1 to Model Rule 5.3 states that lawyers have a duty to ensure that nonlawyer assistants obey ethical rules. The Preliminary Statement to the ABA Model Code notes that the Code defines the ethical conduct expected of lawyers *and* their employees. Because lawyers may be sanctioned for the conduct of their nonlawyer employees, it is imperative that paralegals comply with rules of ethics.

PROHIBITION AGAINST UNAUTHORIZED PRACTICE OF LAW

Paralegals are not allowed to practice law. What constitutes the practice of law is not always clear. Obviously paralegals may not try cases or argue motions. In client conferences and in telephone conversations paralegals obtain information from clients, and clients seek information on the law that applies to their case. As a general rule, persons engage in the practice of law when they apply the law to the particular facts of a client's case. Study the example in the text concerning political asylum.

When in doubt, take the information and the question from the client and submit both to the attorney for an answer. If the attorney cannot personally relate the answer to the client and authorizes you to do so, be sure to tell the client that the opinion is that of the attorney, not your own opinion. It is important that in all phone conversations and written correspondence, both with clients and with others, you clearly identify yourself as a paralegal.

LAWYERS' RESPONSIBILITIES REGARDING NONLAWYER ASSISTANTS

Lawyers must supervise the work of paralegals. This includes a duty to train paralegals regarding the ethical aspects of their employment. One of the most important ethical aspects is the preservation of confidential client information. Another important duty of lawyers is to review the work product of paralegals. Lawyers may delegate work to nonlawyer assistants, but they must supervise that work. Lawyers must maintain a direct relationship with the client and assume complete professional responsibility for the work product of nonlawyer assistants.

Because lawyers may be disciplined for their employees' ethical violations, they have ample incentive to supervise paralegals' work. When lawyers discover that a nonlawyer assistant has engaged in unethical conduct, they must take steps to mitigate the damage.

CONFIDENTIALITY OF CLIENT INFORMATION

One of the most important ethical obligations is to preserve confidential client information. This rule is mandatory. Some information is protected by the attorney-client privilege, which applies in judicial proceedings where an attorney may be called as a witness or asked to produce evidence about the client. The attorney-client privilege protects this information from disclosure.

The protection afforded by the Model Rules and Model Code is broader than the attorney-client privilege. DR 4-101(A) provides that attorneys must protect the "confidences" and "secrets" of clients. "Confidences" refers basically to information protected by the attorney-client privilege—that is, communications between lawyer and client. The definition of "secrets" is broader in scope and includes any information that the client requests be kept inviolate, or disclosure of which would embarrass or be detrimental to the client.

The Model Rules' definition of protected information is even broader. Model Rule 1.6 and its comments indicate that all information gained in the course of representing a client is confidential, whether the information comes from the client or some other source.

The rationale for the confidentiality requirement is that only under guarantee of such protection will clients disclose to their attorneys all information necessary for the case, particularly if the information is embarrassing.

Confidential client information can be shared with other personnel in the law firm. This is necessary to provide adequate representation. However, you should refrain from discussing confidential information more than is necessary to prepare the case adequately. The temptation to gossip about clients is great, but you enhance your professional status by refraining.

Exceptions to the Rule: When an Attorney Can Disclose Confidential Information

Under some circumstances an attorney can disclose confidential client information. The general rules are discussed in the text, but you must know the precise boundaries of the exceptions for your own jurisdiction.

One exception is client consent to disclose information. In the course of litigation some information may be disclosed without contacting the client for permission, and this is known as implied consent. It applies to general facts about the case, such as the name of the manufacturer of the electric blanket in the Wesser case. The comments to Model Rule 1.6 explain that it applies to information "that cannot properly be disputed, or in negotiation . . . facilitates a satisfactory conclusion."

Another exception occurs when a dispute arises concerning a lawyer's conduct, perhaps in the context of a client accusing a lawyer of wrongdoing or a third party accusing both lawyer and client of wrongdoing. Lawyers may disclose confidential information necessary to defend themselves, but no more. One example is a fee dispute in which the attorney may need to explain why representation of a client was more complicated than expected at the outset.

Another exception is to prevent commission of a future crime. This exception applies when a client discloses that he intends to commit a crime in the future. Whereas the Model Code applies this exception to all types of crime, Model Rule 1.6 limits disclosure to crimes that are "likely to result in imminent death or substantial bodily harm." Be sure to determine the version your state has adopted, because some states that in large part adopted the Model Rules retained the Model Code's application to crimes of any sort and rejected the narrower version found in the Model Rules. Remember that this exception applies to future crimes only, not to crimes that have already been committed.

Other ethical rules can override the duty to preserve confidential client information. For example, DR 4-101(A)(4) provides that a lawyer cannot knowingly allow a client to present perjured testimony, even though the information may be confidential. The Model Rules are less specific, but do acknowledge that there are instances when another rule may override the confidentiality requirement. Sometimes a court may order the disclosure of confidential information. Usually the attorney invokes the attorney-client privilege; but if the court insists, the attorney must obey the court order, although the order may first be appealed.

CONFLICT OF INTEREST

Lawyers have a mandatory duty to avoid conflicts of interest. See Model Rule 1.7, DR 5-101 and DR 5-105. A lawyer may not undertake representation of a new client if the representation would be adverse to the interest of a present client. Another context in which conflicts often arise is when multiple parties to a lawsuit want the same lawyer to represent them. The lawyer may represent more than one party to a lawsuit only when the lawyer is certain that this can be done without dividing his or her loyalty and after consent is obtained from the parties. Sometimes the parties' interests are so diverse that the lawyer clearly cannot represent more than one of them. Even when initially it appears that the lawyer may properly represent more than one party, the parties' interests may become divergent later, in which case the attorney must withdraw from the case.

Lawyers have a continuing duty to protect the interests of their former clients and thus cannot represent another person in the same or a substantially related matter when the other person's interests are "materially adverse" to the interests of a former client, unless the former client consents after full disclosure. At no time may a lawyer use confidential information to the detriment of a former client.

Lawyers also have a mandatory duty not to represent a person when the lawyers' own interests prevent them from exercising independent judgment. After they undertake representation, lawyers must also refrain from transactions that may interfere with their independent judgment. Lawyers must limit business dealings where the lawyer and client have differing interests, unless the client consents after disclosure. In addition, lawyers must not exploit to their advantage information relating to the representation of a client.

Every law office needs methods to screen cases to ensure that representation of a person will not create a conflict of interest. The core of such a system is a record of all persons the firm represents or has represented. The check for conflicts may be manual, by checking indices of past and present clients, including the firm's clients and the adverse parties. Many firms use a computer search, which may involve a search of stored documents (pleadings, discovery documents, etc.). Special considerations apply to representation of corporations, because lawyers owe their allegiance to the corporation itself and not to individual officers or stockholders. Lawyers may represent persons connected with the corporations they represent, but only if the lawyer believes that differing interests are not present.

OTHER GENERAL DUTIES TO CLIENTS

Lawyers have a duty to act with reasonable diligence and promptness in representing clients. Because litigators generally have hectic schedules, paralegals play a very important role in keeping the cases moving. Lawyers also have a duty to represent their clients competently. This means that attorneys should not undertake matters in which they do not have sufficient expertise unless they associate another attorney who has the expertise. The duty of competence also encompasses being prepared adequately for trials, depositions, and all phases of litigation. Lawyers also have a duty to communicate regularly with clients and to keep them apprised of all developments in their lawsuit. Paralegals have an important role in communicating with clients by telephone and in maintaining regular written correspondence.

TRANSACTIONS WITH PERSONS OTHER THAN CLIENTS

Lawyers have a duty to be truthful in their statements to the court and to other persons, and this includes the duty not to make a false statement of material fact or law. When lawyers know that a party is represented by counsel, they have a duty to obtain counsel's consent before communicating with that person about any matter related to the litigation. With regard to persons not represented by counsel, the Model Code provides that if the unrepresented person's interests conflict with the lawyer's client's interests, the lawyer may give the person no advice beyond advising him or her to obtain counsel. The Model Rules provide that a lawyer has a duty to inform the unrepresented person that the lawyer is not disinterested in the matter.

CONDUCT SPECIFICALLY RELATED TO LITIGATION

Lawyers have a duty not to advance a "frivolous" claim or defense. Be sure to find out the meaning of "frivolous" in your jurisdiction. Lawyers may not take an action merely for harassment or delay. In addition to the ethics rules, FRCivP 11 requires attorneys to sign pleadings, signifying that they have read the pleadings, that there is good ground for the pleadings, and that they are not being interposed for delay. Lawyers who violate FRCivP 11 may be sanctioned directly by the court, and the sanction may include payment of the other party's attorney's fees generated by the filing lawyer's inappropriate action.

Lawyers have a duty to expedite litigation—that is, to avoid unnecessary delay. Model Rule 3.2 states that the reasonable efforts to expedite shall be consistent with the best interests of the client, and the comment explains that realizing financial gain is not a legitimate cause for delay.

Lawyers also have a duty of candor toward the tribunal, which includes the duty not to knowingly make a false statement to the court or offer false evidence. In addition, attorneys must disclose to the court legal authority in the controlling jurisdiction that is contrary to their clients' position. This means that law unfavorable to the clients' case must be disclosed, and thus paralegals must be sure to include in their legal research cases that do not support their clients' position.

The duty of fairness to the opposing party and counsel requires that lawyers not conceal, falsify, or obstruct access to evidence. This applies to discovery as well as to the trial.

OTHER ETHICAL OBLIGATIONS REGARDING TRIAL CONDUCT

Lawyers must obey the rules of the tribunal. This encompasses the duty to comply with the court's rules of procedure and to comply with the orders the judge enters during the course of the litigation. Lawyers may in good faith contest the judge's orders, but this commonly takes place during the appeal after the final judgment has been entered; in the meantime, lawyers must comply with the orders. Another important trial prohibition is the duty not to communicate with jurors except in formal presentations in the courtroom. Lawyers are not supposed to allude to matters that they do not reasonably believe to be relevent or matters not supported by admissible evidence. DR 7-106 and Model Rule 3.4 contain other prohibitions with which paralegals should be familiar.

Chapter 2   Legal Ethics

STUDY QUESTIONS

1. What are the functions of a state bar?

2. What are the functions of the American Bar Association?

3. What are the two primary models for ethical standards adopted by states?

4. Discuss the three basic components of the ABA Model Code. Explain for each component whether it is a mandatory rule or an aspirational statement of conduct.

5. In the ABA Model Rules, how do you distinguish what is a statement of mandatory conduct?

6. Discuss the types of penalties that can be imposed on lawyers for violating ethical rules.

7. Explain why paralegals must comply with ethical rules of their jurisdiction and the consequences for the attorney if a paralegal fails to comply.

8. What type of activity constitutes the unauthorized practice of law?

9. Explain what lawyers must do to ensure that nonlawyer assistants do not engage in the practice of law.

10. Explain the four primary exceptions to the mandatory rule to preserve confidential client information.

11. May an attorney represent a client whose claim is directly adverse to that of a former client? Why?

12. Explain how a lawyer's own interests might constitute a conflict of interest.

13. What is a lawyer's duty to a potential client if the lawyer perceives a conflict of interest?

14. Once a lawyer undertakes representation of a client, what is the lawyer's duty in regard to business transactions with the client?

15. Discuss methods for screening a potential case for conflicts of interest.

16. Under what circumstances may you communicate with a person represented by counsel?

17. When is a lawsuit considered ''frivolous''?

18. When may an attorney seek an extension of time without violating the duty to expedite litigation?

19. What conduct does the duty of candor toward the tribunal prohibit?

20. How does the duty of fairness to the opposing party guide a paralegal in preparing or answering questions in pretrial discovery?

21. List at least three prohibitions on a lawyer's conduct during a trial.

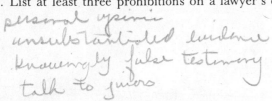

personal opinion
unsubstantiated evidence
knowingly false testimony
talk to jurors

TEST YOUR KNOWLEDGE

MULTIPLE CHOICE

1. Which of the following may paralegals do?

    a. Give legal advice
    b. Draft legal documents
    c. Sign legal documents
    d. None of the above

2. FRCivP 11 requires that attorneys sign all pleadings to signify that:

    a. They believe there is good ground to support the pleading.
    b. They have read the pleading.
    c. The pleading is not filed for the purpose of delay.
    d. a and b only
    e. All of the above

3. Which of the following constitute exceptions to the rule of not divulging confidential client information?

    a. Information necessary to assert a defense to a claim of wrongdoing by the attorney
    b. Information about a client's intent to commit a future crime
    c. Information about a crime already committed by the client
    d. a and b only
    e. All of the above

4. Which of the following groups governs the admission of lawyers to practice law in a state?

    a. The American Bar Association
    b. The state ethics committee
    c. The state bar
    d. None of the above

5. From which of the following must lawyers refrain during trial?

    a. Asserting personal opinions about the honesty of a witness
    b. Communicating with jurors except in formal presentations in the courtroom
    c. Alluding to matters that the lawyer does not believe are relevant
    d. b and c only
    e. All of the above

6. Which of the following state conduct that is mandatory?

    a. The Disciplinary Rules of the ABA Model Code
    b. The Ethical Considerations of the ABA Model Code
    c. ABA Model Rules that use "shall" and "shall not"
    d. a and c only
    e. All of the above

7. Which of the following describe information that must be kept confidential?

    a. "Secrets" as defined in the ABA Model Code
    b. "Confidences" as defined in the ABA Model Code
    c. Under the Model Rules, all information relating to representation
    d. a and b only
    e. All of the above

8. Which of the following accurately describe a lawyer's duty in regard to business transactions with clients?

    a. A lawyer may participate in no business transactions with clients.
    b. A lawyer may not exploit to the client's disadvantage information relating to representation of the client.
    c. A lawyer must refrain from transactions that may interfere with the lawyer's professional judgment.
    d. b and c only
    e. a and c only

9. In which of the following circumstances may a lawyer be subject to discipline?

    a. When the lawyer is directly responsible for the work of a paralegal who engages in conduct that violates ethics rules
    b. When the lawyer is not directly responsible for the work of a paralegal who engages in conduct that violates ethics rules, but the lawyer knows of the conduct and does nothing to stop it
    c. When a paralegal violates ethics rules and the lawyer has not previously advised the paralegal of applicable ethics rules
    d. a and c only
    e. All of the above

10. Which of the following may paralegals sign?

    a. An answer to a complaint
    b. A letter to a client
    c. A motion
    d. None of the above

TRUE/FALSE

1. **T** F   When paralegals sign letters, they must indicate that they are paralegals, not attorneys.

2. T **F**   The duty to preserve confidential client information terminates when a case is closed.

3. **T** F   Paralegals may discuss confidential client information with other persons in the law firm.

4. T **F**   A position is considered ''frivolous'' if that position is unlikely to prevail at trial.

5. T **F**   Legal authority of the controlling jurisdiction that is contrary to your client's position need not be disclosed to the court unless the opposing party brings it up.

6. T **F**   When a lawyer represents more than one party in a matter and a conflict subsequently arises between the parties, the lawyer must withdraw from the case.

7. **T** F   The duty to preserve confidential client information may not be overridden by other ethics rules.

8. **T** F   Lawyers have an ethical duty to educate new employees about ethical rules.

9. **T** F   One rationale for the duty to preserve confidential client information is the necessity that the client tell the lawyer all pertinent information.

10. T **F**   An attorney may not communicate with persons unrepresented by counsel.

11. **T** F   The duty of fairness to opposing parties includes the duty not to conceal evidence.

12. T F   The court may sanction directly lawyers who violate the directives of FRCivP 11.

13. **T** F   Many states have adopted some version of the ABA Model Rules.

14. **T** F   A lawyer may be disciplined for conduct involving fraud or dishonesty.

15. T **F**   The ABA Model Code and Model Rules specify the penalty to be applied for violations of ethics rules.

Chapter 2 Legal Ethics

ANSWERS TO STUDY QUESTIONS

1. The state bar regulates the admission of lawyers to practice in that state. It also controls discipline procedures for lawyers whose conduct breaks the state's ethical rules.

2. One primary function of the ABA is the development of ethical rules, which states may adopt in some form. The ABA puts out legal publications, including the *ABA Journal*. It sponsors continuing legal education courses and works through many committees to better the legal profession.

3. The two primary models on which states base their own ethical rules are the ABA Model Code of Professional Responsibility and the ABA Model Rules of Professional Conduct.

4. The ABA Model Code is divided into nine Canons. Each canon states in broad terms the standards of conduct expected of lawyers. Below each canon are several ethical considerations (ECs) that explain in more detail the broad statements of the canons. The ECs address more specific situations. The disciplinary rules accompanying each canon state mandatory rules and explain the conduct that will subject a lawyer to disciplinary action. The disciplinary rules are mandatory and the ethical considerations are only aspirational in character. The canons are mandatory, although their language is so broad that disciplinary action will more likely be based on a specific disciplinary rule that defines prohibited conduct more definitively.

5. The Model Rules use "shall" and "shall not" to distinguish mandatory conduct. The use of "may" indicates discretionary conduct.

6. The least severe penalty for unethical conduct is a private reprimand, which warns the lawyer in a private letter not to allow such conduct again. A public reprimand warns the lawyer in a statement that is placed in public records. Next in severity is suspension of the right to practice for a designated period. The most serious punishment is disbarment. The severity of the punishment depends on the severity of the misconduct, together with all the circumstances of the case.

7. If a paralegal fails to comply with ethical rules, the lawyer is subject to discipline. Lawyers can also be disciplined if they learn that a paralegal in their firm has broken an ethical rule, but thereafter take no action to correct any damage done by the paralegal's conduct. Thus a paralegal who does not comply with the ethical rules is not a suitable employee for a law firm.

8. The definition of "practice of law" may differ among jurisdictions. A general rule is that a person engages in the practice of law when he or she applies the law to the specific facts of a client's case. Aside from the giving of legal advice, the practice of law also consists of activities such as court appearances. Preparation of a legal document without an attorney's review and signature also constitutes the practice of law.

9. Lawyers have a duty to review the work of paralegals and retain ultimate responsibility for their work product. The lawyer must also maintain a direct relationship with the client. Lawyers must select employees carefully and instruct them as to the limits of their work and their ethical obligations.

10. First, a client may consent to the disclosure of confidential information after the attorney has discussed the consequences of disclosure with the client. This includes implied consent, such as admitting

a fact that is obviously true. The second exception is when a dispute arises about the lawyer's conduct in representing a particular client. This may be in the context of a dispute about the lawyer's fee or when there are allegations of wrongdoing. Third, an attorney may disclose a client's intention to commit a future crime in order to prevent such crime. In some jurisdictions this must be a very serious crime, but in other jurisdictions it includes any crime. A client's admission of a crime already committed is not subject to the exception. Fourth, a disciplinary rule or court order may require disclosure. An example is when an attorney knows a client intends to use false evidence.

11. A lawyer may not represent a client whose claim is directly adverse to that of a former client. One reason is that the attorney may not be able to protect the confidential information of the former client.

12. Attorneys may have personal or financial interests so adverse to the client that they cannot render fair, detached advice.

13. Unless the client consents to representation after full disclosure by the lawyer, the lawyer should decline to represent the client.

14. The lawyer must limit business transactions with the client to those that are fair and must not make use of information gained in the course of representation to the client's disadvantage.

15. A law firm may use a manual method or computer search to check all files and/or documents for names of parties that the firm represents or has represented. Names of adverse parties must also be checked. One method is to check all stored documents for the names of all parties in the new case. Attorneys and paralegals can then review the list generated to determine whether any conflicts of interest exist.

16. You cannot communicate with a person represented by counsel about matters related to the representation unless the person consents or the communication is authorized by law.

17. The definition of ''frivolous'' can vary among jurisdictions. In general, a lawsuit is considered frivolous if it is designed merely to harass or if there is no law to support the merits of the case and no valid argument for changing the law.

18. In the litigation context, a lawyer may seek an extension to file a document or complete a task when there is some purpose besides delay or harassment.

19. The duty of candor toward the tribunal includes the duty to be truthful and to bring forth legal authority in your jurisdiction that is unfavorable to your client if the adverse party has not brought it forth. Lawyers also have a duty to disclose facts necessary to prevent other persons from offering false evidence.

20. Paralegals must remember the duty not to suppress, alter, or obstruct the other party's access to evidence. One must comply with a proper discovery request.

21. Attorneys are prohibited from alluding to any matter that is not relevant or not supported by admissible evidence, and from asserting a personal opinion about a fact in issue unless the lawyer is a witness. Before and throughout the trial a lawyer may not communicate with jurors except during the course of the official trial proceedings. Attorneys may not allow the presentation of false evidence.

ANSWERS TO TEST YOUR KNOWLEDGE

MULTIPLE CHOICE

1. b	6. d
2. e	7. e
3. d	8. d
4. c	9. e
5. e	10. b

TRUE/FALSE

1. T	6. F	11. T
2. F	7. F	12. T
3. T	8. T	13. T
4. F	9. T	14. T
5. F	10. F	15. F

3 COURT ORGANIZATION AND JURISDICTION

SUMMARY

Chapter 3 explains the basic concepts necessary to determine the proper court in which to file a lawsuit. A court can hear a case and render a judgment only if it has jurisdiction. The court must have subject matter jurisdiction, the authority to hear the particular type of action, and personal jurisdiction, the power to bring defendants into court and enter a binding judgment against them.

To apply the concepts of jurisdiction, you must understand the structure of our court systems and master some basic definitions. First, distinguish between trial courts and appellate courts. At the trial court level, the actual trial determines the pertinent facts based on witness testimony, exhibits, and so on. In the event that judgment of a trial court is appealed, an appellate court reviews the proceedings that took place in the trial court and are contained in the record. The appellate court does not hear new testimony but reviews the record of the trial court to determine whether the applicable law was followed and applied.

A court of original jurisdiction is the trial court where a case is commenced and tried. A court of record is a court where a stenographer is present to record the trial court proceedings. Not all trial courts are courts of record.

A court of limited jurisdiction can hear only certain types of cases, as established by statutes. Federal courts are courts of limited jurisdiction. A court of general jurisdiction is not constricted by statute as to what types of cases it can try. State courts are usually courts of general jurisdiction, but a state may have some courts of limited jurisdiction. For example, small claims court may be limited to claims of less than $1,500.

The federal court system has three basic components. The trial courts are the United States district courts. They are courts of limited jurisdiction. Every state has at least one district in its federal court system, and the more populous states have more than one district. The second component consists of the United States courts of appeal, which are appellate courts, reviewing decisions from the United States district courts. These appellate courts are divided into circuits, each of which covers a specified geographical region. The United States Circuit Court of Appeals for the Federal Circuit is an exception in that it hears appeals from certain specified federal trial courts. The United States circuit courts of appeal are also authorized to review decisions of some administrative agencies, as specified by statute.

The third component is the United States Supreme Court, the highest level appellate court in the country. The U.S. Supreme Court is authorized to review decisions of the U.S. circuit courts of appeal and the highest state appellate courts. The U.S. Supreme Court does not have to hear every appeal. Rather, a party must file a petition for certiorari, requesting review by the U.S. Supreme Court. If the U.S. Supreme Court exercises its discretion to review a decision, it issues a writ of certiorari. It often reviews cases where the circuit courts of appeals have reached different conclusions regarding a certain legal issue. At the federal trial court level, there are also some specialized courts, such as the United States Tax Court, whose jurisdiction is constricted by statute to very specific types of cases.

Every state has its own system of state courts, established and governed by that state's constitution and statutes. The trial court system may be split into divisions, often delineated by the dollar amount of the claim. Although most state courts have general jurisdiction, there exist some courts of limited jurisdiction, such as small claims or juvenile court.

Many states have two levels of appellate courts. The intermediate level is often called the court of appeals, and a party may usually appeal to such court as a matter of right—that is, without petitioning the court to exercise its discretion to consider the appeal. However, the highest state appellate court, usually called the state supreme court, generally must approve a petition for discretionary review. The state supreme court hears appeals from the court of appeals and some administrative agencies.

Subject matter jurisdiction determines what type of case a court is authorized to hear. A case may be dismissed at any time if the court does not have subject matter jurisdiction.

Subject matter jurisdiction is a key factor in federal courts, which are authorized to hear only certain types of cases. Many statutes delineate the jurisdiction of the federal courts, but the two most frequently invoked bases of federal jurisdiction are federal question jurisdiction and diversity jurisdiction. Federal question jurisdiction is governed by 28 U.S.C. §1331, which provides that federal courts may hear civil actions ''arising under the Constitution, laws, or treaties of the United States.'' Diversity jurisdiction is governed by 28 U.S.C. §1332. The most common type of diversity case involves citizens of different states. Complete diversity is required; that is, each plaintiff must be a citizen of a different state from each defendant. If one plaintiff is a citizen of the same state of which one defendant is a citizen, complete diversity does not exist. Diversity jurisdiction also requires that the amount in controversy exceeds $50,000. For purposes of diversity jurisdiction, the citizenship of individuals is determined by their domicile, the place where they have their permanent home and intend for their permanent home to remain. A corporation is considered a citizen of the state where it is incorporated and where it has its principal place of business.

A court may have exclusive jurisdiction over certain matters. For example, claims involving Title VII must be filed in federal court. Courts may have concurrent jurisdiction when no statute explicitly states that one court has exclusive jurisdiction over a certain type of case. For example, a personal injury action where diversity jurisdiction exists may be brought in state court, if the plaintiff so chooses.

Personal jurisdiction is the court's power over a defendant—the power to make the defendant litigate in that court. The underlying principle of personal jurisdiction rules is fairness to the defendant. Defendants are entitled to due process—that is, notification that a lawsuit has been filed against them. Most states have long-arm statutes, which delineate circumstances in which an out-of-state defendant has enough contacts within a state to deem litigation fair in that state. Long-arm statutes are founded on the concept of minimum contacts: defendants must have sufficient contacts with the state that their due process rights will not be violated if they are forced to come into that state to defend a lawsuit.

Venue determines in which geographical district an action will be tried. In federal courts venue governs the judicial district in which the trial will be held, and venue in state court usually determines the county for the trial proceedings. The determination of the proper court in which to file an action for purposes of venue is your third consideration after you determine which court has subject matter jurisdiction and whether the court has personal jurisdiction over the defendants.

The first step in the venue analysis is to see whether any special venue statutes apply, specifying the proper judicial district(s). If no special venue statute applies, and the action is filed in state court, check the state's applicable general venue statutes. If the action is in federal court, check the general federal venue statute, 28 U.S.C. §1291.

To determine venue, you must look at the residence of the parties. According to 28 U.S.C. §1391(a), in actions based on diversity jurisdiction, venue is proper in the district where all plaintiffs reside, all defendants reside, or the cause of action arose. In actions not based on diversity jurisdiction, 28 U.S.C. §1391(b) states that venue is proper where all plaintiffs reside or where the cause of action arose. An individual's residence for purposes of venue is based on domicile. A special rule for corporations is provided in 28 U.S.C. §1391(c). For purposes of venue, a corporation is a resident of any judicial district in which it is subject to personal jurisdiction at the time the action was commenced. Defendants may file a motion for a change of venue if they feel venue is improper. If venue is not proper, the court may either dismiss the action or transfer it to a judicial district where venue is proper. Courts generally choose transfer over dismissal.

Chapter 3 Court Organization and Jurisdiction

STUDY QUESTIONS

1. Why is it imperative to determine which court has jurisdiction to hear your lawsuit?

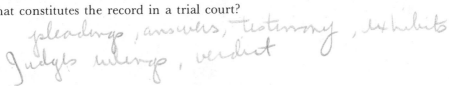

judgment not binding in court that does not have jurisdiction

2. What constitutes the record in a trial court?

pleadings, answers, testimony, exhibits judges ruling, verdict

3. On what does an appellate court base its decision? How is this different from the trial court?

brief oral argument points of law

trial court on evidence, etc.

4. In which reporter can you find judicial decisions from the United States district courts? From the circuit courts of appeal?

F. Supp

F. F. 2d Federal Reporter

5. Explain the types of cases the United States Supreme Court has power to decide.

any appeal chosen
points of law
differences in circuits

6. Name two specialized federal trial courts.

Tax
Court of Claims

7. Explain the difference between an appeal and a trial *de novo*.

de novo new trial evidence, etc.

8. Explain the types of issues that support federal question jurisdiction.

9. Most lawsuits based on diversity jurisdiction involve controversies between what types of parties?

parties from different state

10. How do you determine the citizenship of a corporation for purposes of diversity jurisdiction?

main office citizen / domicile

11. Why must a court have personal jurisdiction over a defendant?

order to court / order to perform

12. If an action is filed in a United States district court, how does the court determine whether a long-arm statute applies?

due process

13. If a state's long-arm statute applies to a defendant, but a court determines that sufficient minimum contacts to protect the defendant's right to due process do not exist, is the plaintiff left without recourse?

try where cause of action or where defendant lives

14. How do you determine the proper venue for a lawsuit in federal court?

circuit

15. What alternative does a court have when it determines that venue is not proper?

transfer or dismiss usually transfer

TEST YOUR KNOWLEDGE

MULTIPLE CHOICE

1. Trial courts are courts of _____*original*_____ jurisdiction.

   a. appellate
   b. nominal
   c. personal
   d. original

2. United States district courts are courts of _____*limited*_____ jurisdiction.

   a. limited
   b. general
   c. appellate
   d. nominal

3. Subject matter jurisdiction in the United States district courts may be based on _____*d*_____.

   a. federal question jurisdiction
   b. diversity jurisdiction
   c. an issue involving patent law
   d. All of the above

4. When both state and federal courts are authorized to hear a certain type of action, _____*a*_____ jurisdiction exists.

   a. concurrent
   b. personal
   c. exclusive
   d. None of the above

5. In a federal court action based on diversity jurisdiction, venue is proper in the district where
   _____*d*_____ .

   a. all plaintiffs reside
   b. the cause of action arose
   c. all defendants reside
   d. All of the above

6. Judicial opinions from the United States Courts of Appeal are published in _____*b*_____ .

   a. *Federal Supplement*
   b. *Federal Reporter*
   c. *Code of Federal Regulations*
   d. All of the above

7. Jurisdiction for lawsuits involving employment discrimination claims under Title VII may be filed in _____ a _____ .

   a. United States district court
   b. the state trial court where the cause of action arose
   c. United States Court of Appeals
   d. Both a and b, because concurrent jurisdiction exists

8. The United States Supreme Court is empowered to hear which of the following?

   a. Cases involving a controversy between states
   b. Decisions of the United States Courts of Appeal
   c. Decisions of the states' highest courts
   d. All of the above

9. Federal question jurisdiction applies to which of the following?

   a. Any controversy that involves an amount exceeding $50,000
   b. Employment discrimination claims based on federal statutes
   c. Allegations of violations of due process under the U.S. Constitution
   d. All of the above
   e. b and c only

10. Which of the following are courts of limited jurisdiction?

   a. Federal trial courts
   b. Small claims courts
   c. State trial courts
   d. All of the above
   e. a and b only

TRUE/FALSE

1. T F   For purposes of venue, a corporation is considered a resident of a judicial district if the court in the district can obtain personal jurisdiction over the defendant corporation.

2. T F   The District of Columbia is in the Fourth Circuit Court of Appeals.

3. T F   An appeal from an administrative agency decision can never go directly to a circuit court of appeals.

4. T F   If the United States Supreme Court declines to review a decision of a circuit court of appeals, the decision of the circuit court of appeals stands as the final decision.

5. T F   Most of the highest state appellate courts have discretion to pick the decisions they will review.

6. T F   For purposes of diversity jurisdiction, a corporation may be considered a citizen of only one state.

7. T (F) For purposes of diversity jurisdiction, to determine whether the jurisdictional amount is met, you look to the defendant's answer to determine whether an amount in excess of $50,000 is at issue.

8. T F After a plaintiff files a complaint in a court, the plaintiff may later assert that the court has no personal jurisdiction over the plaintiff.

9. T (F) In regard to personal jurisdiction, a defendant has no right to due process.

10. (T) F If a state's long-arm statute provides personal jurisdiction over a defendant, the defendant must still receive adequate notice of the lawsuit.

11. T (F) The purpose of the venue requirement is to ensure fairness to the plaintiff.

12. (T) F Small claims courts are courts of limited jurisdiction.

13. (T) F When a transcript of a trial is made, the court is called a court of record.

14. T (F) State courts are all courts of general jurisdiction.

15. T (F) All judicial decisions generated by the United States circuit courts of appeal are published.

Chapter 3   Court Organization and Jurisdiction

ANSWERS TO STUDY QUESTIONS

1. Because a case may be dismissed at any point in the litigation if the court does not have jurisdiction.

2. The testimony given at the trial, the pleadings, the discovery documents (depositions, interrogatories, etc.), exhibits introduced at trial, and other documents from the litigation at the trial level.

3. The trial court hears the testimony of the witnesses and considers the documents presented at trial as exhibits, as well as pleadings and discovery documents, all of which comprise the record. At trial the judge, or the jury in a jury trial, determines the facts and applies the applicable law to reach a verdict. The appellate court reviews the record from the trial court and no new testimony. The appellate court reviews the record to determine whether the law was properly applied and the judge states a basis for the result reached by applying the law to the facts.

4. United States district court decisions appear in *Federal Supplement* (F. Supp.). Decisions from the circuit courts of appeal are in *Federal Reporter* (F., F.2d).

5. The U.S. Supreme Court is authorized to hear appeals from the U.S. circuit courts of appeal and from the highest-level state appellate courts. In addition to hearing appeals, the U.S. Supreme Court has original jurisdiction over very few types of cases, such as controversies between two states.

6. United States Court of Claims and United States Tax Court.

7. A trial *de novo* is a complete new trial, in which witnesses testify again. An appellate decision is based on the record—that is, the proceedings in the trial court; the appellate court does not hear new testimony or consider new exhibits. The appellate court reviews the record "below" for errors; it does not conduct a new trial.

8. Federal question jurisdiction exists when a lawsuit involves issues arising under the Constitution, laws, or treaties of the United States. Thus the action may involve a constitutional right or a federal statute, such as Title VII.

9. Citizens of different states.

10. For purposes of diversity jurisdiction, a corporation is considered a citizen of the state where it has its principal place of business or headquarters and where it is incorporated.

11. If a court does not have personal jurisdiction over a defendant, it cannot make the defendant litigate in the forum state and cannot enter a binding judgment against the defendant.

12. The court first considers whether there is an applicable federal long-arm statute. If there is no federal statute, the court examines the long-arm statute of the state in which the federal court sits.

13. No. The plaintiff may sue the defendant in the state where the defendant resides. The courts in the defendant's state of residence do have personal jurisdiction over the defendant.

14. First you check to see whether there is a special venue statute that applies. If no special federal statute applies, use the general federal venue statute, 28 U.S.C. §1391.

15. The court may dismiss the action or transfer it to a district where venue is proper. Courts usually prefer to transfer rather than dismiss.

ANSWERS TO TEST YOUR KNOWLEDGE

MULTIPLE CHOICE

1. d   6. b

2. a   7. a

3. d   8. d

4. a   9. e

5. d   10. e

TRUE/FALSE

1. T   6. F   11. F

2. F   7. F   12. T

3. F   8. F   13. T

4. T   9. F   14. F

5. T   10. T   15. F

4 EVIDENCE

SUMMARY

Chapter 4 presents the basic principles of the rules of evidence. The rules of evidence determine which evidence is admissible, that is, which evidence the finder of fact may consider in reaching a verdict. Evidence includes testimony of witnesses, generally called testimonial evidence, and documents, generally called documentary evidence. Parties may also present physical objects, referred to as physical or real evidence. Evidence is direct when a witness has firsthand knowledge of the facts. Evidence is circumstantial when it is not based on personal observation. Direct evidence generally carries more weight. Do not be unduly concerned about categorizing by type every piece of evidence. Rather, keep in mind the general principles of evidence to determine when evidence is admissible.

Our discussion focuses on the Federal Rules of Evidence, published in the United States Code and in commercial publications. In state court, apply that state's rules of evidence, which can be found in the state statutes and commercial publications. You may also refer to various books about evidence, because the application of the rules is not always clear. Remember that state rules of evidence may have significant differences from the federal rules.

The rules of evidence have two primary purposes: to ensure fairness and to ascertain the truth. Ensuring fairness is the requirement that evidence be relevant. Ensuring truthfulness is the requirement that evidence be reliable.

FRE 402 states that only relevant evidence is admissible to resolve the issues in a lawsuit. Evidence is relevant when it tends to prove the existence of a fact that is important to the outcome of the dispute. The evidence must have a logical bearing on the issues in dispute. It need not prove the ultimate issue in dispute; background information to understand the ultimate issue is important.

Even relevant evidence may be excluded under certain circumstances. FRE 403 provides that relevant evidence may be excluded when its probative value is outweighed by the danger of prejudice, confusion, or misleading the jury; or by considerations of undue delay, waste of time, or needless presentation of cumulative evidence. The court weighs these dangers against the probative value to determine whether evidence is admissible, and great discretion is exercised in making this decision.

Character evidence is evidence of a person's reputation in the community or evidence of a particular trait. Often character evidence is not relevant. The general rule in civil litigation (FRE 404) is that character evidence is not admissible to establish that the person acted in conformity with the trait on a particular occasion. Character evidence is admissible when a person's trait is an element of a claim or defense, such as in a defamation case. This does not occur often. It is important to distinguish between character evidence to show a person acted in conformity with a trait, and character evidence of a person's truthfulness or untruthfulness, used to impeach (discredit) the witness's testimony. For instance, if a person has been convicted of a crime that involves dishonesty, such as embezzlement, character evidence may show that a person is not generally truthful.

Distinguish evidence of habit, which is generally admissible. Habit is a person's consistent response to a particular situation, not evidence of that person's general traits, as character evidence is. We assume that if a person reacts to a certain situation in the same way every time, she or he likely reacted that same way during the event in question.

The Federal Rules of Evidence have other specific rules regarding relevance. FRE 407 provides that evidence that remedial measures were taken after an accident is not admissible to prove negligence. The public policy behind this rule is that we do not wish to create a disincentive for persons to remedy dangerous situations. FRE 408 states that offers to settle a dispute are not admissible to show liability. The rationale here is to encourage settlement discussions. FRE 409 provides that evidence of paying or promising to pay medical expenses is not admissible to prove liability for the injury. FRE 411 provides that evidence as to whether a person had liability insurance is not admissible to show that a person acted negligently. The rationale for these rules is to avoid creating a disincentive to tender assistance for medical expenses or to keep liability insurance.

Several rules of evidence are designed to ensure reliability. Witnesses must take an oath that they will tell the truth (FRE 603). A very important requirement is that witnesses have personal knowledge of the matters about which they testify (FRE 602). At trial, lawyers ask witnesses questions to show that they have personal knowledge of the facts about which they testify. This is known as laying a foundation.

Lay witnesses (as distinguished from expert witnesses) may state their opinions about questions in dispute, if they have observed the facts on which they base their opinions. According to FRE 701, opinion testimony by lay witnesses is allowed when it is rationally based on the perception of the witness and is helpful to a clear understanding of the witness's testimony or the determination of a fact in issue. Thus witnesses cannot come into court and state their opinions simply because they happen to have opinions about an issue in dispute.

In contrast, expert witnesses are allowed to state opinions based on other persons' observations. The requirement for expert testimony is that the opinion be based on facts of a type reasonably relied on by experts in that particular field. Before witnesses can testify as experts, they must be qualified as experts. An expert witness must have sufficient knowledge, skill, experience, training, or education to explain and give an opinion about technical subjects that average lay persons generally do not understand. For example, the average person does not know enough about electrical malfunctions to know what caused the electric blanket in the Wesser case to catch on fire. However, a person with sufficient knowledge about electrical wiring and design knows enough to state an opinion about the cause of the fire. To determine whether a person is qualified to be an expert witness, you review education, experience, and other credentials. Paralegals often research the background of the other parties' experts as well as their own.

If a witness's testimony is inconsistent, the testimony may not be reliable. One way to attack the reliability of testimony is to attack the witness's credibility. This is known as impeachment. Several factors may indicate that a person is not telling the truth. A person may give contradictory and inconsistent statements or have a bias—that is, a motive for not telling the truth. For instance, a witness's family or business relationship with a party may influence his or her testimony. Another impeachment device is to show that a person is untruthful, and here character evidence can be used. Distinguish this from the use of character evidence to show a person acted in conformity with a trait during an event in question. If a person has been convicted of embezzlement, character evidence may show that the person is dishonest and unlikely to tell the truth. It does not, however, establish that the person is bad and therefore must have committed a negligent act.

There are two rules designed to ensure that documents are reliable. The first is the requirement that all documents be authenticated. To authenticate a document, the person presenting the document must establish that the document is what is purports to be. For example, in a contract dispute, the person introducing the contract into evidence must establish that this is the contract that the parties entered. At trial, attorneys generally authenticate by asking the witness whether, for instance, "this is the contract which you and the defendant entered." FRE 901 allows lay persons to identify signatures. A common way to authenticate documents that are public records, such as deeds, is to have an official in the office where the record is kept certify the document as a true copy. For instance, an employee in the office of the Register of Deeds can certify that a deed is a true copy of the deed recorded in that office. FRE 902 sets forth several types of documents that are self-authenticating, that is, documents deemed on their face to be authentic without further proof. Examples are certified copies of public records, such as the deed discussed above, and newspapers.

The second rule for documents is the original writing rule (FRE 1002). This is sometimes called the best-evidence rule. The rule requires that when the content of a document is in issue, the original of the document must be produced, unless the original is unavailable or unless another evidence rule or statute permits submission of a copy. FRE 1003 permits submission of a duplicate in many circumstances. FRE 1003 allows use of a duplicate unless a genuine question is raised as to the authenticity of the original or it would be unfair to admit the duplicate in lieu of the original.

The hearsay rule is also designed to ensure reliability. Hearsay is testimony in court about a statement made out of court, where the out-of-court statement is offered to prove the truth of the matter asserted in the out-of-court statement. If a statement is hearsay, it is not admissible to prove the truth of the content of the statement unless the statement fits into an exception to the hearsay rule. The hearsay rule is designed to prevent one person from coming into court and testifying about what another person said, when that other person is not available for cross-examination. Cross-examination is the primary means of testing the truthfulness of a statement.

There are many exceptions to the hearsay rule, as set out in FRE 803 and 804. The exceptions in FRE 804 require that the declarant (the person who made the out-of-court statement) be unavailable for trial. A person may be dead or too ill to attend. The witness may not be able to remember the subject matter of the statement, or the court may not be able to secure the witness's presence.

One frequently encountered exception to the hearsay rule is the excited utterance, where a person is so excited when making a statement that she would not have had time to fabricate it. Statements made to a doctor for diagnosis or treatment also form an exception, because we assume that a person tells a doctor the truth in order to receive proper treatment. Many types of public records fall within the hearsay exceptions (FRE 803(8) through (17)). We accept the documents' trustworthiness because they are regularly kept by agencies such as the Register of Deeds.

If a person is unavailable for trial, testimony given at another hearing or in a deposition fits the exception in FRE 804(b)(1). A person's statement against interest is also an exception, because we assume that persons will not say things to their detriment unless the things are true.

Our last major topic in evidence is privileges. Privileged communications are statements that are protected from forced disclosure because the statements were made between persons who have a confidential relationship with each other. The Federal Rules of Evidence do not address specific privileges. Rather, you must consult the applicable statutes and case law. In state court, consult the state's statutes and case law. In a federal court case, where jurisdiction is based on diversity, look to the statutes and case law of the state in which the court sits. If federal jurisdiction is based on subject matter jurisdiction, you apply the privilege rules developed by the federal courts.

Privilege rules are important at every stage of litigation. Paralegals must be constantly alert lest they unwittingly disclose privileged information. In particular, paralegals should screen documents for privileged information before releasing them to another party. Note potentially privileged matters and discuss them with the attorneys on your team.

One frequently encountered privilege is the attorney-client privilege, which protects confidential communications between clients and their attorneys. A communication is confidential when it is not intended to be heard by a third party. For example, discussions in the attorney's office are likely to be confidential, and the presence of persons on the attorney's staff does not destroy confidentiality. But if an attorney and client discuss a matter in a crowded bar where they know that people can overhear them, their communications are not confidential. In addition, the purpose of the communications must be to render legal advice. Discussion of last night's baseball game or the weather are not for the purpose of rendering legal advice, unless questions about the weather or the baseball game are at issue.

Note that confidential communications include documents such as letters from attorneys to clients. The attorney-client privilege attaches to confidential communications from the very beginning of the meeting to get legal advice. The privilege protects the communications even after the attorney has closed the client's file.

There are exceptions to the attorney-client privilege. For example, statements to the attorney concerning future crimes or fraud that the client intends to commit are not privileged. Information necessary to resolve a dispute between an attorney and a client is not privileged. When disputes arise between joint clients, the information the attorney gained while meeting with the parties together is not privileged. For other exceptions, consult the law in your jurisdiction.

Clients may waive the attorney-client privilege by voluntarily sharing the information with third parties. The attorney may not waive the privilege for the client. Only the client can waive it.

Another important privilege is the work product privilege (FRCivP 26(b)(3)). An attorney's mental impressions, conclusions, and opinions on legal theories are absolutely protected. A qualified privilege attaches to documents ''prepared in anticipation of litigation'' by a party's ''representative,'' such as a report prepared for the attorney by an insurance investigator. The other party may obtain the information only if the party has a ''substantial need'' and cannot obtain a ''substantial equivalent'' of the documents ''without undue hardship.'' The terms within quotes are open to interpretation, so you must check the law in your jurisdiction.

The husband-wife privilege protects confidential communications between husband and wife. The presence of third parties will destroy confidentiality. Only communications made during a valid marriage are included. The husband-wife privilege does not apply in cases involving crimes against a spouse or the children of either spouse, or in lawsuits between the spouses.

Another privilege recognized in most jurisdictions is the physician-patient privilege, which protects information that a doctor obtains in treating a patient. Patients frequently waive this privilege, as when they sign authorizations for the physician to release their medical records in personal injury litigation.

Other privileges exist in certain jurisdictions: a journalist's informants, government secrets, an accountant's records. As with other privilege rules, you must consult the law of the proper jurisdiction.

Chapter 4   Evidence

STUDY QUESTIONS

1. Describe the three major types of evidence.

2. What is the difference between direct and circumstantial evidence?

3. Explain the meaning of ''admissible'' evidence.

4. Explain the term ''finder of fact.''

5. Where can you find the Federal Rules of Evidence and explanatory notes about them?

6. Explain briefly the two primary goals of the Federal Rules of Evidence and how these goals are accomplished.

7. State the general requirements for evidence to be considered relevant.

8. According to FRE 403, when may evidence be excluded even though it is relevant?

9. When is character evidence admissible in civil litigation?

10. How does evidence of habit differ from character evidence?

11. Why is evidence of remedial repairs after an accident not admissible to show that a dangerous condition existed?

12. Discuss two requirements in the rules of evidence to ensure that witnesses give reliable testimony.

13. Under what circumstances may lay witnesses state their opinions about issues in dispute?

14. Explain the two requirements for expert witnesses to give admissible testimony.

15. Are expert witnesses allowed to base their opinions on facts or data determined by other persons?

16. Discuss three methods to impeach a witness.

17. Explain the methods to authenticate a document and why authentication is required.

18. Explain whether the original writing rule ever allows the submission of a duplicate of a document.

19. Explain the definition of hearsay and the rationale for the hearsay rule.

20. Explain three common exceptions to the hearsay rule.

21. What are the sources for rules that govern privileges?

22. Explain why privileges are so important.

23. Explain the type of information to which the attorney-client privilege applies.

24. How is the attorney-client privilege waived?

25. Discuss three exceptions to the attorney-client privilege.

26. What are the two basic requirements for the husband-wife privilege to apply?

27. How do patients waive the physician-patient privilege?

TEST YOUR KNOWLEDGE

MULTIPLE CHOICE

1. Which of the following may show that a witness is biased?

   a. Close family relationship to a party
   b. Business relationship to a party
   c. Long-standing grudge against a party
   d. a and b only
   e. All of the above

2. Which of the following are exceptions to the hearsay rule?

   a. Testimony at a prior hearing
   b. Statements against interest
   c. Excited utterances
   d. b and c only
   e. All of the above

3. Which of the following is necessary for the testimony of an expert witness to be admissible?

   a. The testimony must assist the finder of fact to understand a fact in issue.
   b. The expert must have personal knowledge of the data on which the testimony is based.
   c. The expert must have advanced university degrees.
   d. None of the above

4. Relevant evidence may be excluded when

   a. it is hearsay that does not fit an exception to the hearsay rule.
   b. the witness does not have personal knowledge of the fact.
   c. the risk of unfair prejudice outweighs the probative value.
   d. All of the above
   e. a and c only

5. Which of the following does the attorney-client privilege protect?

   a. Communications about crimes the client has already committed
   b. Communications made by the client when only the attorney and paralegal are present
   c. Communications necessary to resolve disputes between attorneys and clients
   d. a and b only
   e. None of the above

6. Which of the following statements about the work product privilege is false?

   a. The privilege affords only qualified protection to the mental impressions of attorneys.
   b. Documents prepared in anticipation of litigation may be protected by the work product privilege.
   c. A memorandum by the attorney outlining trial strategy would be protected by the work product privilege.
   d. All of the above

7. Which of the following aims to ensure that evidence is reliable?

   a. The hearsay rule
   b. The requirement of personal knowledge
   c. The requirement that an expert be qualified as an expert
   d. a and b only
   e. All of the above

8. Which of the following may be used to impeach a witness?

   a. Bias
   b. Prior inconsistent statements
   c. Evidence that the witness is dishonest
   d. All of the above
   e. a and b only

9. Which of the following statements about authentication of documents are true?

  a. The parties may stipulate to the authenticity of documents before trial.
  b. Some documents are self-authenticating.
  c. A witness may at trial identify a document as being authentic.
  d. All of the above
  e. a and b only

10. Which of the following methods could be used to authenticate Sandy Ford's signature on the employment application?

  a. Ask Sandy Ford to identify the signature.
  b. Ask the personnel manager, who saw Ford sign the application, to identify the signature.
  c. Have the defense attorney stipluate that the signature is Sandy Ford's signature.
  d. a and c only
  e. All of the above

TRUE/FALSE

1. T F   A certified copy of a public document is self-authenticating.

2. T F   A witness is considered "unavailable" for purposes of FRE 804 if the witness cannot remember the subject matter of the statement made out of court.

3. T F   The attorney-client privilege may be waived by the attorney on behalf of the client.

4. T F   Admissions of a party opponent are not hearsay under the Federal Rules of Evidence.

5. T F   Hearsay evidence is confined to testimony.

6. T F   Business records kept in the regular course of business constitute an exception to the hearsay rule.

7. T F   In a lawsuit involving defective car brakes, an automobile mechanic may qualify as an expert witness.

8. T F   Prior inconsistent statements may be used to impeach a witness at trial.

9. T F   The testimony of any witness may be impeached.

10. T F   The Federal Rules of Evidence define all the privileges that paralegals may encounter.

11. T F   In order to be considered relevant, evidence must address the ultimate fact in dispute.

12. T F   Direct evidence is generally more persuasive than circumstantial evidence.

13. T F   Lay witnesses are allowed to identify signatures and voices.

14. T F   The original writing rule does not allow the submission of duplicates of documents.

15. T F   Evidence that parties engaged in settlement discussions is never admissible.

Chapter 4 Evidence

ANSWERS TO STUDY QUESTIONS

1. Testimonial evidence is the testimony of witnesses. Documentary evidence consists of the documents submitted as exhibits. Real, or physical, evidence consists of objects that the jury can see and handle, such as an electric blanket.

2. Direct evidence is based on a person's firsthand knowledge of the facts about which the person testifies. Circumstantial evidence is not based on personal observation; rather, the witness infers a conclusion about the fact in dispute. Direct evidence is generally more persuasive.

3. Admissible evidence is evidence that the judge determines may be introduced at trial and considered by the finder of fact.

4. The finder of fact determines from the evidence presented at trial which facts are true. In a jury trial, the jury is the finder of fact. In a nonjury trial, the judge is the finder of fact.

5. The Federal Rules of Evidence are published in the U.S. Code and in commercial publications. The annotations in U.S. Code Annotated provide short explanations of judicial decisions interpreting the rules of evidence. Treatises such as *McCormick on Evidence* also help with application of the rules to fact situations.

6. One primary goal is to ensure fairness to all parties. This goal is accomplished by the requirement that evidence be relevant. The second primary goal is to ascertain the truth. This goal is attained by the requirement that evidence be reliable.

7. In order to be relevant, evidence must help the finder of fact understand the ultimate fact. The evidence need not answer the ultimate fact; it is sufficient if it provides the background necessary for understanding the ultimate issue in dispute. Evidence must have a tendency to establish a fact of consequence. It must also have a logical bearing on the dispute.

8. Relevant evidence may be excluded when its probative value is outweighed by the danger of unfair prejudice or confusion of the issues, or is misleading. When relevant evidence causes undue delay, waste of time, or needless presentation of cumulative evidence, it may also be excluded. Great discretion rests with the judge in weighing these factors.

9. Evidence of a person's reputation in the community or of a particular trait may not be used to show that a person acted in conformity with his reputation or trait on a particular occasion. This would constitute substantive evidence, but such evidence is deemed not to be relevant.

   Distinguish the use of character evidence to impeach a witness. You may introduce evidence of a person's truthfulness or untruthfulness. For example, if a person has been convicted of a crime involving dishonesty, this may show that the person is not truthful. This serves as impeachment evidence only. It does not serve as substantive evidence that a person who would commit such a crime probably acted a certain way on a certain occasion.

10. Character evidence refers to a person's general traits. Evidence of a person's habits shows a consistent response to a particular situation. We assume evidence of a habit is relevant to show that a person always responds in a certain way in a certain situation.

11. There is a public policy consideration. The rationale for this rule is to avoid creating an incentive *not* to make needed repairs.

12. First, witnesses must take an oath that they will tell the truth. This reminds the witness of the duty to tell the truth.

    Second, witnesses must have personal knowledge of the facts about which they testify. Witnesses' testimony is bound to be more reliable if they are limited to facts about which they have personal knowledge.

13. Witnesses may state their opinions when the opinions are rationally based on the witnesses' perception and the opinions are helpful to a clear understanding of their testimony or the determination of a fact in issue. The concepts of both reliability (personal observation) and relevance (helpfulness toward understanding) are embodied in this requirement.

14. First, the subject matter must be appropriate for expert testimony. This means that the expert's testimony must concern scientific, technical, or other specialized knowledge that will assist the trier of fact to understand the evidence or to determine a fact in issue. Such testimony will help lay persons understand technical matters.

    Second, expert witnesses must be qualified as witnesses. A person may qualify as an expert based on knowledge, skill, experience, training, or education, or a combination of these factors.

15. Yes. FRE 703 allows expert witnesses to base their opinions on observations of other persons. In fact, the evidence on which they base their opinions does not even have to be admissible.

16. Impeachment is an attack on a witness's credibility. One method of impeachment is to point out contradictory and inconsistent statements the witness has made. It is important for paralegals to be alert constantly for inconsistencies. A second method of impeachment is to show that the witness is biased—that is, has a motive for being untruthful. Bias may be caused by a close family relationship, business relationship, or a grudge against a party. Character evidence may be used for impeachment. Evidence to prove that a person is untruthful may be used for impeachment.

17. Authentication of documents is necessary to ensure their reliability. The parties may agree that certain documents are authentic and then they do not have to prove authenticity at trial. One method to prove authenticity at trial is to have a witness identify the document as being what it purports to be, such as Sandy Ford's employment application. Lay witnesses are allowed to identify signatures, if they are familiar with a person's signature.

    Certain documents are deemed to be self-authenticating under the Federal Rules of Evidence. When a document is self-authenticating, it is accepted as authentic on its face and evidence that it is genuine need not be presented at trial. An example of a self-authenticating document is a certified copy of a public record.

18. FRE 1002 provides that to prove the content of a writing (or a recording or photograph), the original is required unless another rule of evidence or statute allows submission of a copy, or the original cannot be found. This applies when the content of the document is in issue. FRE 1003 allows submission of a duplicate in many instances. Specifically, it allows submission of a duplicate unless a genuine question is raised as to the authenticity of the original or it would be unfair to admit the duplicate in lieu of the original.

19. Hearsay is testimony in court about a statement made out of court, where the out-of-court statement is offered to prove the truth of the matter asserted in the out-of-court statement. For example, if a witness testifies that another person said that the light was red, this is hearsay if it is offered to prove that the light was red.

The hearsay rule provides that if evidence is hearsay, it is not admissible unless it fits into an exception to the hearsay rule. The purpose of the rule is to ensure that the person who made the out-of-court statement can be cross-examined. Cross-examination is used to test the witness to see whether he or she is telling the truth. Bias may also be shown by cross-examination.

20. One exception is the excited utterance. The rationale behind this exception is that the person is so excited that she has not had time to fabricate a story.

    Another common exception is business records kept in the regular course of business. The rationale here is that the records were kept for business purposes, not for litigation purposes, and that the business would want accurate records.

    Another common exception is former testimony of a witness at another trial or hearing, or at a deposition. The rationale here is that the witness was under oath when he gave the former testimony and thus told the truth.

21. The Federal Rules of Evidence do not provide specific rules for privileges. You must look to the statutes and case law of your state when your lawsuit is in state court. In federal court, your source depends on the type of federal jurisdiction you assert. If you have diversity jurisdiction, you look to the rules developed by the courts in the state in which the federal court sits. When you rely on subject matter jurisdiction, you look to the rules developed by the federal courts.

22. Paralegals must be alert for privileged information at every stage in the litigation process. If you do not recognize that information is privileged, you will unwittingly disclose privileged information to the opposition.

23. The attorney-client privilege protects from forced disclosure confidential communications between clients and their attorneys. Communications are confidential if they are not intended to be heard by third persons. However, the presence of the attorney's employees does not destroy the privilege. In addition to being confidential, the communications must also be made for the purpose of obtaining legal advice. Communications may be oral or written.

24. The client may waive the protection of the attorney-client privilege by voluntarily disclosing the protected information to third parties. Only the client may waive the privilege. The attorney may not waive the privilege on the client's behalf.

25. One exception is information about crimes that the client intends to commit in the future.

    Another exception involves disputes between attorneys and their clients. This usually arises in the context of disputes over attorneys' fees. An attorney may disclose information necessary to resolve the dispute, but should be careful not to disclose any more information than is necessary.

    A third exception can occur when an attorney has undertaken representation of multiple parties to a lawsuit. If the parties' interests later diverge and their interests become adverse, communications made to the attorney when they all met together are not protected by the attorney-client privilege.

26. The communications between husband and wife must be confidential—that is, not intended to be shared with third parties. Second, the communications must take place during the course of a valid marriage. Thus communications before parties are married are not protected by the husband-wife privilege.

27. Patients often sign authorizations for doctors to release medical records. For instance, in personal injury litigation, the client's attorney needs the client's medical records. Patients can waive the privilege by making statements in the presence of third parties. The presence of the doctor's staff does not waive the privilege, but the presence of other persons may result in waiver. The law may differ among jurisdictions.

ANSWERS TO TEST YOUR KNOWLEDGE

MULTIPLE CHOICE

1. e	6. a
2. e	7. e
3. a	8. d
4. d	9. d
5. d	10. e

TRUE/FALSE

1. T	6. T	11. F
2. T	7. T	12. T
3. F	8. T	13. T
4. T	9. T	14. F
5. F	10. F	15. F

5 DEVELOPMENT OF THE CASE

SUMMARY

The object of Chapter 5 is to understand the steps in the litigation process from the time you open a client's file through the informal investigation stage. We must develop our case before preparing the complaint and commencing the lawsuit.

Our first topic is opening and organizing files. We discuss the general procedures, but it is important to remember that different law firms have different procedures. At the outset you should understand the necessity of keeping a master list of the files assigned to you. List the client name, file number, and general status of the case. Attorneys in the firm keep master lists of the cases assigned to them also.

You may not be the person in your firm who actually opens the file, but you must understand the procedure. The first step is to complete a case opening sheet. This contains the basic information you need to identify and contact your client and the other parties or their attorneys, if they are represented. Remember that when your client is a corporation you have a contact person there. Include the contact person's name, address, and phone number.

After the case opening sheet is completed, the file is routed to the appropriate clerical personnel, who enter the information in the computer system. This is important for maintaining an index of the firm's clients and for maintaining records for billing. The firm may also keep a manual index of client information. Before routing the file, be sure that all documents already obtained are put in the file. Throughout the litigation process, remember the importance of preserving all evidence, including original documents.

The next topic is file organization. This is important because a common duty of paralegals is to maintain the voluminous documents in a file in an orderly manner. A standard format is the large, rigid file container housing subfiles in manila folders. Subfile methods may vary from one firm to another, but the important goal is to find documents quickly.

A common subfile category is court papers: the pleadings and other documents filed with the court. If discovery materials are filed with the court, they may be kept in this subfile unless they are too bulky. This subfile also contains the orders and judgment entered by the court.

Another common category is correspondence with court and counsel: letters to the court and to the attorneys representing the other parties. A subfile for general correspondence contains letters to and from the client and letters to obtain information from other persons. Correspondence is generally arranged in chronological order. If the litigation is protracted, you may have to split the correspondence into separate subfiles according to years.

Another subfile category is file memoranda. This includes memos the attorneys and clients write to record information, such as the content of conversations with clients and others. Still another category is legal research: copies of pertinent judicial opinions and memos summarizing the results of legal research.

A subfile may be set up for memoranda of law, commonly called briefs. In simple cases, the memoranda of law may be included with court documents, since they are filed in support of motions.

Discovery materials often fill up several subfiles. If you undergo extensive discovery in a lawsuit, you may need very specific subfiles, such as Plaintiff's First Set of Interrogatories to Defendant Second Ledge.

Another subfile may be set up for the lawyers' notes; such notes may outline legal theories or the results of factual research. Paralegals may also need subfiles for their notes. You can create a subfile for news clippings, if there are any concerning your lawsuit or related matters.

A common subfile is billing matters. It contains receipts for out-of-pocket expenses and perhaps the individual time slips filled out for work on that case.

Indexing files is an important task often assigned to paralegals. A given law firm may use one of several indexing systems, but the goal remains to find documents quickly. Sometimes an index in the front of the main file is sufficient. However, in complex cases, you may need an index in the front of each subfile. Describe the documents in each subfile specifically. Include dates if necessary to avoid confusion, especially for correspondence subfiles. In pleadings subfiles, it is common to attach a tab to the side of each document to provide ready identification.

Many law firms have a central file area where they store the original documents. Originals must be examined or copied in the central storage area, and often can be removed only if they are formally checked out. The purpose is to lessen the risk of losing original documents. For their everyday work, attorneys and paralegals use the working files, which contain copies of the documents. The organization and indexes for the central file and working file should be uniform.

Our next step is to analyze the remedies available to our client. There are two major categories of remedies—money damages and equitable relief. There are two primary types of money damages. The first is compensatory damages, which aim to make the party whole by payment of an amount to compensate the client for personal injury or property damage. Compensatory damages are often divided into special damages and general damages. Special damages are awarded for items of loss that are specific to the particular plaintiff, such as lost wages due to injury. General damages are awarded as compensation for less tangible losses, such as pain and suffering.

The second primary type of money damages is punitive damages. These are sometimes called exemplary damages. Punitive damages, as the name implies, are intended to punish defendants for egregious conduct and to make examples of them. Punitive damages are awarded in addition to compensatory damages and frequently amount to three times the amount of compensatory damages.

Equitable remedies are appropriate when the plaintiff's loss cannot be compensated by monetary damages. A frequently encountered equitable remedy is the injunction, a court order for a party to refrain from a certain action. Sometimes a party must be stopped from taking an action for which the damaged party could not be compensated monetarily, such as the loss of a 100-year-old oak tree.

Another common equitable remedy is specific performance. This remedy arises in contract disputes. A court can order a party to perform the action that it promised to do in the contract. This remedy is appropriate when the object in question is unique, such as real estate or a priceless painting that one party promised to sell.

Another remedy is the award of attorney's fees. The important point is that each party must pay its own attorney's fees unless a statute gives the court authority to order one party to pay the other party's attorney's fees. Certain types of statutes contain an attorney's fee provision, such as civil rights actions or alimony actions.

Our next step is to organize the informal investigation. Our first step is to chart the essential elements of each claim. We then decide how to obtain the information necessary to prove the essential elements of each claim. Recall that an essential element is a fact that the law requires to exist in order to establish a particular cause of action.

Next identify all defendants. Take special care to designate correctly corporate defendants. The company may be a subdivision of another company, and the names may be confusing. It is important to join all defendants. The goal is to adjudicate all claims in one lawsuit. It would be confusing and wasteful to adjudicate the claims against one defendant in one lawsuit and then repeat the entire process against another defendant in a second lawsuit. FRCivP 19 requires that all parties who are "united in interest" should be joined in the lawsuit.

At every stage of litigation, including informal investigation, consider the rules of evidence. Your goal is to avoid wasting time on evidence that is unlikely to be admissible at trial.

Next we must determine the sources of information for the facts we must prove. The sources vary, depending on the subject matter of the lawsuit. If you need ideas for sources, talk to the other paralegals and lawyers in the firm, and examine similar files.

Your first source of information is the client. Find out as much general information as you can about what happened. Obtain all pertinent documents that the client can supply. Also find out names of potential witnesses. Obtain personal background on your clients—age, education, occupation, salary, assets, and family history. Observe a client's demeanor to determine whether the client will be a good witness.

You can also obtain information from potential witnesses. Building upon the facts obtained from the client, determine the specific information you want from the witness. Get information about the witness's personal background.

Documents are an important part of the evidence in most lawsuits. Determine the documents you need and where you can obtain them. If the opposing side has the documents, you may have to obtain them through the discovery process. Other persons with pertinent documents may voluntarily share them with you.

Next, consider whether there is pertinent physical evidence, such as the electric blanket in the Wesser case. Get possession of physical evidence as soon as possible, and strive to preserve it in its condition at the time the claim arose. If it cannot be preserved in that condition, take photographs.

Next, determine whether you need expert witnesses. They are not necessary in every lawsuit, but are frequently used in personal injury litigation. There are many methods for locating experts. Start in your law firm by asking the attorneys and other paralegals for recommendations. If that fails, consult with attorneys and paralegals in other firms. You may also review advertisements in professional publications, such as the *ABA Journal*. Sometimes you use experts to review the file early on to assess the claim, even if you do not use that expert at trial.

Now that we have planned the evidence we need, we must obtain it. The method we use depends on the nature of the information we need. Interviews of both clients and witnesses are helpful methods for obtaining facts. Prepare for interviews by determining what you already know and what information the person can provide for you. You may prepare a checklist of questions. Next, arrange the interview. This is easy with clients. They can come to your office at a mutually convenient time. Arranging to interview witnesses may be more of a challenge; some may not want to talk with you at all or may grudgingly agree to talk if you keep the exchange short. On the other hand, you may have to pay them a surprise visit and hope for the best.

When you conduct the interview, strive to put the person at ease. Avoid interruptions such as telephone calls. Remember that some persons will never before have had contact with attorneys and paralegals, and they may feel intimidated. Promptly record the content of the interview. You may sometimes take notes at the interview, or ask the witness for permission to tape-record the interview. If you do neither, it is imperative that you write down the content of the conversation immediately afterward. Be sure the attorneys on your team get a copy.

Physical evidence must be obtained and preserved promptly. You may obtain it from the client or from another source, such as an insurance adjuster. Preserve its condition, if possible. If this is not possible, take photographs. If you keep the evidence, label it and place it in a protective container. If you must let someone else borrow the object, record this in a log.

Frequently you will need to obtain large numbers of documents. Your sources will vary according to the types of documents you need. If the documents you seek are confidential, such as medical or personnel records, obtain signed authorization from the client to release the information. Check with the person or institution to determine whether they have special authorization forms you must use and whether they have any special procedures. Also ask how much they charge for copies. This can save you time and expense. Once you receive the documents, review them immediately. Determine whether you received everything you requested. Your review of the documents may also alert you to other documents that you need to obtain.

Chapter 5 Development of the Case

STUDY QUESTIONS

1. Explain the purpose of a case opening sheet and the information usually contained on it.

2. Why is the information on the case opening sheet usually entered into the firm's computer system?

3. What documents besides the case opening sheet are usually put in a newly opened file?

4. Describe at least five subfile categories frequently used in litigation files.

5. Explain where indexes to subfiles are generally kept.

6. Explain the difference between central and working files.

7. After a complaint is filed, may a party add further claims for relief later?

8. Explain the types of money damages.

9. Explain the purpose of punitive damages and the general amount usually awarded.

10. Explain when equitable remedies are appropriate. Include an explanation of at least one example of equitable remedies.

11. When is an award of attorney's fees allowed?

12. Explain the meaning of ''essential elements'' and how an informal investigation can be organized on the basis of essential elements.

13. Why is it important to determine all defendants at the beginning of the informal investigation?

14. Under the Federal Rules of Civil Procedure, may the court order that parties be added or severed from a lawsuit?

15. Why is it important to consider the rules of evidence during the informal investigation?

16. What are the four primary sources of evidence?

17. Discuss at least four types of information that paralegals should obtain from clients in a personal injury lawsuit.

18. What types of information may paralegals obtain from other witnesses besides the client?

19. Why is it important to preserve the condition of physical evidence at the time of the accident?

20. How can you show the condition of the physical evidence if it must be repaired before trial?

21. In what types of lawsuits are expert witnesses often used?

22. Describe methods for locating expert witnesses.

23. Discuss techniques for conducting successful interviews.

24. How may you obtain information or documents from unwilling witnesses?

25. How may paralegals record the content of interviews?

26. Explain how to obtain a person's medical records or employment records.

TEST YOUR KNOWLEDGE

TRUE/FALSE

1. T F   Copies of documents are usually kept in working files, while originals are usually kept in central files.

2. T F   The manner in which files are organized may differ among law firms.

3. T F   The client contact may differ from case to case, especially if your client is a corporation.

4. T F   Information from case opening sheets may be used for docket control and for screening conflicts of interest.

5. T F   Indexes to subfiles are always found in one large index on the inside front cover of the outside file.

6. T F   Checklists are useful for preparing for interviews.

7. T F   Discovery subfile categories may differ, depending on the bulk of the materials.

8. T F   Lost wages are a type of general damage.

9. T F   An injunction is a type of compensatory damage.

10. T F   In most lawsuits attorney's fees are awarded to the prevailing party.

11. T F   Specific performance is an appropriate remedy when one party contracts to sell a unique
            item but then refuses to sell.

12. T F   The Federal Rules of Civil Procedure encourage separate lawsuits against multiple defen-
            dants, in order to avoid confusion.

13. T F   Because employment records are confidential, you will need an authorization to release
            if you are to obtain them.

14. T F   Expert witnesses may be used to assess a claim early in the litigation process without
            testifying at trial.

15. T F   Expert witnesses are necessary in all personal injury litigation.

16. T F   It is not advisable to begin an interview by allowing a client to tell the story in his or
            her own words.

17. T F   It is necessary to obtain personal background information from clients but not from other
            witnesses.

18. T F   Correspondence is usually arranged in chronological order within subfiles.

19. T F   Physical evidence may be obtained from an opposing party only through the formal
            discovery process.

20. T F   Judges may order that parties be added as defendants, regardless of whether the plaintiff
            named the parties as defendants.

Chapter 5   Development of the Case

ANSWERS TO STUDY QUESTIONS

1. The purpose of a case opening sheet is to compile the basic information to identify the parties to the lawsuit and how to contact the parties or their attorneys. The content of case opening sheets may differ among firms, but certain information is commonly included. First appear the names of the parties and the file number assigned to the file by the law firm. Next come the address and phone number of the client. The contact person may have to be designated, especially if the client is a corporation. Next is the name, address, and phone number of the opposing party's attorney. Next is information used internally by the firm. This includes the names of the attorney and paralegal responsible for the case. The case opening sheet usually has a space to record the person who referred the person to the law firm. The case opening sheet also has a place to record the date the file was opened and the date it was closed. The sheet also indicates the type of fee arrangement.

2. It is important to have a record of the names of all parties in order to check for conflicts of interest. Also, much of the information on the sheet is needed for billing purposes—client's name and address, fee arrangement, and so on.

3. If a written fee agreement has been signed, it goes in the file. Any notes and memos, such as notes from the initial client conference, are put in the file. Any documents received from the client must also be put in the file.

4. One subfile is court papers, pleadings and motions filed with the court together with supporting documents. This subfile also contains orders and the judgment entered by the court. When a case is simple and the discovery materials are required to be filed with the court, the discovery materials may be included.

   Another common subfile is correspondence with the court and attorneys for the other parties. All other correspondence may be kept in a subfile labeled "other correspondence." Correspondence is generally kept in chronological order. In complex cases, the correspondence may have to be further divided by year and/or person.

   File memoranda may be a subfile. Memos range from synopses of interviews to notes regarding trial strategy. File memoranda frequently contain summaries of facts that attorneys and paralegals share with one another. A separate subfile is often kept for legal memoranda, or briefs. In fact, briefs are sometimes kept in the court papers file.

   Discovery materials may be kept in one subfile or several subfiles, depending on the size of the materials. In more complex cases, several subfiles are necessary. It is crucial to label the subfiles specifically: for example, "Plaintiff's Second Set of Interrogatories to Defendant Second Ledge."

   The fruits of legal research may comprise one subfile. Another common category is a subfile for the lawyers' handwritten notes. Newspaper clippings may be in a separate subfile. Finally, a subfile may contain billing information, such as receipts for out-of-pocket expenses or individual time slips.

5. The method of indexing may differ depending largely on the size of the file. One index on the inside cover of the rigid outside file may be sufficient. However, in larger files, an index on the inside of each subfile may be necessary.

6. Original documents are stored in central files, and the documents can either be copied in the central file area or checked out briefly. The purpose of a central file system is to prevent the loss of original

documents. Working files contain copies of the original documents. Attorneys and paralegals use the copies for their daily work and can make notes on them.

7. Generally, parties can add more grounds for relief by amending their pleadings. Sometimes court permission is necessary to amend.

8. Compensatory damages, as the name implies, compensate a party with money for the harm caused by another party. An example is payment for property damage to a home. Compensatory damages are generally classified as either general or special damages. Special damages are specific to a party, such as the party's lost wages or medical expenses. Special damages can generally be measured with precision, because of the "concrete" nature of the damages. General damages are for less tangible losses, such as pain and suffering, temporary or permanent disfigurement, and temporary or permanent disability. There is no specific formula for calculating the amount due for these less tangible damages. In contrast to the precision of doctor and hospital bills to measure medical expenses, pain and suffering has no precise documentary proof.

9. Punitive (sometimes called exemplary) damages are designed to punish a person who has committed some particularly egregious act. The purpose of punitive damages is to punish the persons and make examples of them. Punitive damages are awarded in addition to compensatory damages, not in place of them. Punitive damages may equal three times the amount of the compensatory damages.

10. Equitable remedies are designed to make whole an injured party when money damages cannot compensate the party. An example of an equitable remedy is an injunction, which is a court order directing a party to refrain from certain conduct. If persons are preparing to destroy an object that cannot be replaced or adequately compensated with money, an injunction is appropriate to prevent the destruction. A person in danger of irreparable harm generally seeks an injunction. Another type of equitable remedy is specific performance, which is appropriate when a party contracts to sell a unique item and then refuses to sell it. An example would be a piece of real estate or a priceless painting. The object cannot be replaced with a like object, so it is appropriate for the court to order the person to fulfill the terms of the contract by selling the unique item.

11. The general rule is that parties have to pay their own attorney's fees. A party that loses a lawsuit can be ordered to pay the attorney's fees of the prevailing party only when a statute allows the court to order the award of attorney's fees. Examples of statutes allowing the award of attorney's fees are civil rights, alimony, child support, and consumer protection laws.

12. Essential elements are the facts that the law requires to exist in order to establish a particular cause of action. A party can prevail on a claim only when the party can prove each essential element of that claim. It is important to remember that a party must prove every essential element of every claim against every party. It is helpful to draw a chart showing the essential elements of each claim against each party. Under each essential element, you can list the information you need and the likely source for that information. This will make it obvious if you are lacking some crucial information.

13. The Federal Rules of Civil Procedure encourage the resolution in one lawsuit of all claims arising out of the same transaction or occurrence. If there were two defendants, it would be a waste of time and money to try the case against one defendant and subsequently repeat the same evidence in a trial against the other defendant. FRCivP 19 requires that all parties "who are united in interest"

be joined in the lawsuit. This means that all parties necessary for a complete determination of the dispute must be joined.

14. The Federal Rules of Civil Procedure allow both. The court may order that parties be added if they are needed for a complete resolution of the dispute. Although the rules encourage joining all necessary parties, if this would be unduly confusing, the court may order the severing of a party to a separate lawsuit.

15. It is important to consider whether evidence will be admissible at trial. If a piece of evidence is almost certainly inadmissible, it is advisable to look for another way to prove the fact that the piece of evidence concerns.

16. The four primary sources are clients, witnesses, physical and documentary evidence, and expert witnesses. These are not the only types of acceptable evidence, but most evidence falls within these categories.

17. Paralegals should obtain the basic facts from the client. Then paralegals should address the more specific topics of possible witnesses, the types of injuries the client suffered, where the client received medical treatment, and the client's personal background—job, salary, education, marital status, and so on.

18. A paralegal may elicit the pertinent facts that the witness knows and the identity of other potential witnesses. Paralegals may also obtain documentary or physical evidence that witnesses will voluntarily share. Paralegals should take care to obtain facts about witnesses' personal background.

19. Physical evidence may prove the cause of damages or the amount of damages. For instance, in a car accident, the condition of the car right after the accident may indicate who was at fault by showing where the car was hit. The condition of the car may help to show the amount of work necessary to repair the car. In the case of a plane crash, the ''black box'' may reveal the cause of the crash.

20. The condition may be shown by photographs.

21. Expert witnesses are often used in personal injury litigation, such as product liability and medical malpractice. However, experts are not necessary in every personal injury lawsuit.

22. The starting point is to ask attorneys and paralegals in your law firm. Next, you may ask attorneys and paralegals in other firms. Trial lawyer associations publish information about experts, and experts place advertisements in professional publications, such as the *ABA Journal*.

23. One of the most important things is to help the interviewee feel at ease. Listen carefully to the person, and do not allow interruptions such as phone calls. Prepare for the interview beforehand, so you will know the questions you need to ask. Checklists may be helpful to ensure that you obtain all necessary information.

24. During the informal investigation, the witnesses must volunteer the information and documents. If witnesses are unwilling to cooperate during the informal investigation, you may subpoena them for deposition during the discovery phase and order them to bring specified documents to the deposition. However, it is more helpful if you can persuade a witness to cooperate early on.

25. Paralegals need the interviewees' permission to tape-record their conversation. Paralegals may take notes during the interview. If paralegals do not wish to take notes during the interview, they should dictate or write a memo recording the content of the interview immediately after the interview is over.

26. Both medical records and employment records are considered confidential. Therefore the person must sign an authorization requesting that the custodian of the records release the records to the law firm. Before sending a letter requesting the records, it is advisable to contact the employer or provider of medical services to determine if any special procedures are required—the use of certain authorization forms, for example. Inquire also about the cost of the copies and whether you are to send a check with the request or wait for the custodian to send you a bill. Prepare a letter specifying the exact records you need, and send it along with the authorization.

ANSWERS TO TEST YOUR KNOWLEDGE

TRUE/FALSE

1. T	6. T	11. T	16. F
2. T	7. T	12. F	17. F
3. T	8. F	13. T	18. T
4. T	9. F	14. T	19. F
5. F	10. F	15. F	20. T

6 COMMENCEMENT OF THE PLAINTIFF'S LAWSUIT

SUMMARY

Chapter 6 explains how to prepare the documents necessary to commence a lawsuit. The first document is the complaint, which is the first pleading filed and which explains the plaintiff's claim for relief. Before preparing a complaint, it is necessary to review the general rules that apply to all pleadings. FRCivP 7 states the various types of pleadings that are allowed. FRCivP 8 states the general rule for the content of pleadings—that is, that pleadings must provide a "short and plain statement of the claim." This is the concept of notice pleading, which means that parties plead in a clear, concise manner the reasons why they are entitled to relief, but need not state every detail. Rather, FRCivP 8 requires enough detail to allow the other parties to prepare a defense.

Next, you must understand the basic format requirements for pleadings, which are set forth in FRCivP 10. All pleadings require a caption and numbered paragraphs. The discussion in the text and the illustrations show how a completed complaint looks. Pleadings must be signed by the attorney of record in accordance with FRCivP 11, which states that attorneys' signatures indicate that they have reviewed the facts and law and are not filing a frivolous pleading or a pleading filed only to delay the litigation. Clients have to sign a verification of the facts in a pleading only in limited circumstances, such as when they are also seeking a temporary restraining order or when a state law requires client verification in certain types of state court actions.

FRCivP 3 provides that the filing of a complaint commences the lawsuit. A complaint must contain three substantive elements—a statement of jurisdiction, a statement of the claims, and the demand for judgment. Statements of jurisdiction are illustrated in Figures 6-1, 6-5, and in the Wesser and Chattooga complaints in the Appendix. The statement of the claim must explain the plaintiff's cause of action—that is, a claim for which a court can grant relief. Not every perceived wrong constitutes a cause of action. To state successfully a cause of action, one must plead the essential elements of the claim—that is, the facts that the law requires to exist in order to establish a particular cause of action. The demand for judgment states the types of relief the plaintiff seeks, including monetary damages, equitable relief, attorney's fees, and so on. Finally, the attorney signs the complaint, and the paralegal checks to be sure all necessary exhibits are attached.

The next document to prepare is the summons, which is the form that accompanies the complaint and informs the defendants that they have been sued and within how many days they must file a response. Another document that accompanies the complaint in federal actions is the civil cover sheet. This is a preprinted form on which you check the type of action you are filing and other details that help the clerk to keep track of the litigation.

Service of process is the delivery of the summons and complaints to the defendants in accordance with FRCivP 4. Proper service of process is necessary to gain personal jurisdiction over defendants. FRCivP 4 has technical provisions as to how and on whom process can be served. Options for the manner of service include service by mail, including the notice and acknowledgment method; personal service by a person who is not a party to the lawsuit; and service by a United States marshal. The person on whom service can properly be made depends on the type of defendant. Different subsections of FRCivP 4(d) apply depending on whether the defendant is or is not an infant or incompetent; a corporation, partnership, or other unincorporated association; the United States; an agency or officer of the United States; or a state or municipal corporation or other governmental organization that is subject to suit.

In federal court actions, if service of process is not accomplished within 120 days of the filing of the complaint, the complaint may be dismissed as to the unserved defendants. Service of process in state court actions may be subject to different technicalities concerning deadlines for service and manner of service, depending on the state rules of civil procedure. State long-arm statutes often provide for substituted service on nonresident defendants.

The actual mechanics of filing a lawsuit include taking to the clerk of court's office the complaint, summons, filing fee, and civil cover sheet. The clerk assigns a civil file number, stamps the complaint "filed," and issues the summons. Be sure to take sufficient copies of all documents. Then arrange for service of process. After service has been made, file proof of service with the clerk. This can be done by filing the summons with the completed return of service on the back, or filing a separate affidavit with other proof of service, depending upon how service was accomplished.

At the commencement of a lawsuit, the plaintiff may need injunctive relief if she or he faces a situation involving immediate and irreparable harm for which money damages are insufficient. The plaintiff first requests a temporary restraining order, which orders the defendant to refrain from the harmful activity. A TRO is commonly issued for 10 days, at which time a hearing is held on whether a preliminary injunction should issue. A preliminary injunction prevents the harmful activity until a trial can be held.

A final topic to consider is the class action. This type of lawsuit is designed to allow a large group of persons with similar grievances to bring one lawsuit on behalf of themselves and other persons with the same grievance. The rules for certifying a class action are technical and are set forth in FRCivP 23.

Chapter 6   Commencement of the Plaintiff's Lawsuit

STUDY QUESTIONS

1. Define "pleadings." What is the first pleading filed in a lawsuit?

2. Explain the meaning of notice pleading.

3. What elements must the caption of a pleading contain?

4. Where can you find guidelines for the format and content of pleadings?

5. What precautions must you take when using forms for pleadings?

6. What are the three substantive elements that Rule 8(a) of the Federal Rules of Civil Procedure requires in every complaint?

7. Explain the meaning of the ''essential elements'' of the claim and why it is important to allege all the essential elements in a complaint.

8. Why are separate causes of action alleged in separate sections of a complaint?

9. When attorneys sign a pleading, what do they signify that they have done?

10. When an exhibit is attached to a complaint, how do you refer to the exhibit?

11. What goes in the complaint after the demand for judgment?

12. How does the clerk of court ''issue'' a summons?

13. How do you determine whether special additional forms must be filed with the complaint?

14. What does service of process mean and which Federal Rule of Civil Procedure governs it?

15. With service by mail, how many days must you wait for receipt of the acknowledgment form from the defendant? If the defendant does not respond within the allotted period, what must you do?

16. If you cannot serve the defendant by mail, what other methods of service are acceptable?

17. Who receives the summons and complaint when the defendant is an individual who is not an infant or incompetent?

18. Who receives the summons and complaint when the defendant is a corporation?

19. When you file a lawsuit in federal court, what documents and items must you take to the clerk's office?

20. What Federal Rule of Civil Procedure governs temporary restraining orders and preliminary injunctions, and what must a party show for entry of a TRO or preliminary injunction?

21. What is the purpose of a class action?

TEST YOUR KNOWLEDGE

MULTIPLE CHOICE

1. The Federal Rules of Civil Procedure allow which of the following as pleadings?

    a. Complaint
    b. Answer
    c. Answer to counterclaim
    d. a and b only
    e. All of the above

2. FRCivP 10 requires which of the following in a pleading's caption?

    a. Name of court
    b. File number
    c. Address of defendants
    d. a and b only
    e. All of the above

3. Which of the Federal Rules of Civil Procedure governs the method used for service of process?

    a. FRCivP 4
    b. FRCivP 7
    c. FRCivP 8
    d. FRCivP 10

4. Which of the following are proper methods for service of process on a corporation?

    a. Delivery of summons and complaint to the corporation's authorized agent for service of process
    b. Mailing summons and complaint, together with notice and acknowledgment, to the corporation's authorized agent for service of process
    c. Delivery of summons and complaint to the secretary of state
    d. a and b only
    e. All of the above

5. A preliminary injunction

    a. usually lasts 10 days only.
    b. extends the relief granted by a temporary restraining order.
    c. usually lasts until trial on the issues.
    d. b and c only
    e. All of the above

6. In a complaint, the demand for judgment

    a. is sometimes called the "prayer for relief."
    b. must state each type of relief the plaintiff requests.
    c. may include alternative forms of relief.
    d. All of the above

7. A summons

    a. informs defendants that they have been sued.
    b. informs defendants how many days they are allowed for filing a response.
    c. is the pleading that commences a lawsuit when it is filed.
    d. a and b only
    e. All of the above

8. When the defendant is a federal agency, service of process must include

    a. delivery of summons and complaint to U.S. Attorney's office.
    b. service of summons and complaint by certified mail on U.S. Attorney General.
    c. service of summons and complaint by certified mail on the agency being sued.
    d. a and c only
    e. All of the above

9. Proof of service may in general be shown by

    a. completion of the Return of Service on the back of the summons.
    b. filing an affidavit as to service by certified mail.
    c. phoning the clerk's office to inform them that service has been completed.
    d. a and b only
    e. All of the above

10. A client must verify a complaint

    a. when seeking a temporary restraining order at the time the complaint is filed.
    b. when state law requires verification.
    c. Never
    d. a and b only
    e. All of the above

TRUE/FALSE

1. T F   FRCivP 23 governs class actions.

2. T F   The Federal Rules of Civil Procedure are based on the concept of notice pleading.

3. T F   The civil cover sheet must be served on the defendants in order to commence a lawsuit.

4. T F   It is improper to hire a person to serve process.

5. T F   A group of plaintiffs may institute a class action so long as their claims are similar.

6. T F   The purpose of a civil cover sheet is to help the clerk of court keep track of litigation.

7. T F   The name and address of a corporation's authorized agent for service of process may generally be obtained from the office of the secretary of state.

8. T F   In a lawsuit filed in federal court, service of process must be accomplished within 60 days of filing the complaint, or the action may be dismissed as to unserved defendants.

9. (T) F   In state court actions, the sheriff of the county in which the defendant resides may serve process.

10. T (F)   A request for a temporary restraining order may not be filed until 10 days after the filing of the complaint.

11. (T) F   A lawsuit is commenced in federal court by filing a complaint.

12. T (F)   State rules of civil procedure are always the same as the Federal Rules of Civil Procedure.

13. (T) F   A claim for which a court can fashion relief is called a cause of action.

14. T (F)   A plaintiff's request for a jury trial may be implied and need not be expressly stated in the complaint.

15. T (F)   Any wrong that a person suffers constitutes a cause of action.

Chapter 6   Commencement of the Plaintiff's Lawsuit

ANSWERS TO STUDY QUESTIONS

1. Pleadings are the formal documents filed in a lawsuit, in which the parties set forth their claims and defenses. The first pleading filed in a lawsuit is the complaint.

2. Notice pleading means that a party asserts in pleadings only sufficient facts to give the other party fair notice of the party's claims and defenses. The Federal Rules of Civil Procedure are based on the concept of notice pleading. Thus Rule 8 requires only a "short and plain statement of the claim showing the pleader is entitled to relief."

3. The caption of a pleading contains the name of the court, the title of the action (the designation of the parties), the name of the pleading (e.g., "complaint"), and the file number (civil action number).

4. You can find guidelines for the format and content of pleadings in the Appendix of Forms that appears at the end of the Federal Rules of Civil Procedure in 28 United States Code. Your state rules of civil procedure may contain an appendix of forms. You can also examine files in your office and pleadings filed in the clerk's office.

5. When using forms to draft pleadings, be sure to tailor the form to the particular facts of your case. Do not rely on pleadings that the court dismissed for failure to state a claim for relief.

6. Rule 8(a) requires in every complaint a statement of jurisdiction, a short and plain statement of the claim, and a demand for judgment.

7. The essential elements of a claim or cause of action are the facts which the law requires to exist in order to establish a particular cause of action. A complaint states a claim on which relief can be granted by a court only when the complaint alleges all the essential elements of a particular cause of action. If a plaintiff does not sufficiently allege the essential elements of his claim, his complaint will be dismissed or will have to be amended.

8. Separate causes of action are alleged in separate sections of a complaint so that all the claims on which the plaintiff relies for recovery will be clear to the court.

9. By signing a complaint, attorneys signify that they have read the pleading and made "reasonable inquiry" into the law and the facts of the case and have determined that there is a sound basis in fact and in law for the pleading and that the pleading is not interposed for delay.

10. When an exhibit is attached to a complaint, you state that document "X" is attached as Exhibit A and incorporated into the complaint.

11. After the demand for judgment comes the signature of the attorney, together with his or her address and phone number. This is followed by the verification page, if verification is required.

12. The clerk issues a summons by signing and dating the summons, stamping it with the court seal, and filling in the civil case number.

13. You can determine special forms that must be filed with a complaint by checking the local court rules and asking attorneys and paralegals in your firm. You can also ask employees in the clerk's office.

14. Service of process means delivery of the summons and complaint to the defendants. It is governed by Rule 4 of the Federal Rules of Civil Procedure.

15. You must wait 20 days for receipt of the ackowledgment form. If the defendant does not respond within 20 days, you must attempt service of process by one of the other methods in Rule 4(c).

16. A person who is not a party to the lawsuit and is not less than 18 years of age may serve the summons and complaint. In addition, the courts may order service by a U.S. marshal or a person specially appointed to serve process.

17. When the defendant is an individual who is not an infant or incompetent, the summons and complaint are served on the defendant or are served by leaving copies at the defendant's dwelling place or usual place of abode with a person of suitable age and discretion who resides there or upon an agent authorized by appointment or by law to receive service.

18. When the defendant is a corporation, the summons and complaint are delivered to an officer, a managing or general agent, or to any other agent authorized by appointment or by law to receive service of process.

19. To file a lawsuit in federal court, take the original complaint and sufficient copies, the original summons and sufficient copies, the civil cover sheet, a check for the filing fee, and Form USM-285 if a U.S. marshal is to serve the summons and complaint.

20. Federal Rule 65 governs TROs and preliminary injunctions. Parties must establish that they will suffer immediate and irreparable harm and that money damages cannot compensate them.

21. Class actions allow a large number of persons with similar grievances to participate in one lawsuit rather than initiating hundreds or thousands of separate lawsuits.

ANSWERS TO TEST YOUR KNOWLEDGE

MULTIPLE CHOICE

1. e	6. d
2. d	7. d
3. a	8. e
4. d	9. d
5. d	10. d

TRUE/FALSE

1. T	6. T	11. T
2. T	7. T	12. F
3. F	8. F	13. T
4. F	9. T	14. F
5. F	10. F	15. F

7 SUBSEQUENT PLEADINGS

SUMMARY

In Chapter 6 we examined the first pleading in a lawsuit, the complaint. Chapter 7 explains the pleadings filed after the complaint—the answer, the counterclaim, the cross-claim, and the third-party complaint. FRCivP 7 also allows replies to counterclaims and answers to cross-claims. Not every one of these pleadings is filed in every lawsuit. However, you need to be familiar with all of them. Chapter 7 also explains motions to dismiss pursuant to FRCivP 12. Although technically denominated motions rather than pleadings, these motions are often filed as part of an answer so they must be addressed at this stage of the litigation.

The timing for filing responses to pleadings is critical, and keeping track of the deadlines is a task often assigned to paralegals. The first task is to determine how long applicable statutes allow for filing a response. FRCivP 6 states the rules for calculating response times. There is no substitute for reading FRCivP 6 carefully and applying the stated rules precisely. Note the differences in calculation, depending whether the time allowed to respond is less than 11 days or more than 11 days. Note also that three extra days are allowed when the pleading to which you must respond was served by mail.

Sometimes it is not possible to file a responsive pleading within the allotted time, and the attorney/paralegal team must seek an extension of time. Often counsel for the opposing party will consent to an extension, and the parties file a stipulation or consent order stating their agreement. Otherwise, one must obtain court permission. If the prescribed period has not expired, one must establish "good cause" for an extension. If the prescribed period has already expired, one must establish that failure to file a timely response was the result of "excusable neglect."

FRCivP 12(b) provides seven grounds on which to seek dismissal of a lawsuit: lack of subject matter jurisdiction, lack of personal jurisdiction, improper venue, insufficiency of process, insufficiency of service of process, failure to state a claim upon which a relief can be granted, and failure to join a party under FRCivP 19. These motions must be filed within the time allowed to file the answer and may be part of the answer or filed as separate motions. Certain of the 12(b) motions must be included with the answer or a motion to strike, or else the right to assert the defenses is waived. Review the rules in FRCivP 12(g) and (h) and the discussion on page 165 of the text.

Many of the defects attacked by Rule 12 motions can be cured. This is true of the most commonly asserted motion—failure to state a claim upon which relief can be granted (FRCivP 12(b)(6)).

FRCivP 12(e) addresses the motion for a more definite statement. This motion is filed when the pleading to which you must respond is so vague that a party cannot reasonably be required to frame a responsive pleading. This motion is not appropriate every time you discern a fact you may need to know later, because that is the purpose of the discovery process. However, if the pleading is so vague that you cannot formulate a response without risking an unwanted admission, a motion to strike is appropriate.

FRCivP 12(f) addresses the motion to strike. The purpose of this motion is to strike from a pleading material that is scandalous, unnecessary, and prejudicial.

A topic of paramount importance is the answer, the general rules for which are set forth in FRCivP 8. The general rules of pleading discussed in Chapter 6 apply to answers. The main purpose of the answer is to admit or deny the allegations in the complaint. FRCivP 8 requires that the defendant admit or deny every averment in the complaint. If a defendant is without sufficient knowledge or belief as to the truth of an averment, the defendant may so state, and this is deemed a denial. A failure to respond to an allegation is considered an admission, so it is imperative that the defendant respond to every allegation. A defendant may admit in part and deny in part an averment.

In addition, the answer may contain affirmative defenses, which go beyond a denial and introduce new material that may bar the plaintiff's claim. Common examples of affirmative defenses are statute of limitations, contributory negligence, and the others named in FRCivP 8(c). An answer may also include Rule 12 motions to dismiss, counterclaims, and cross-claims.

The format is similar to complaints, with numbered paragraphs, headings, prayer for relief, and attorney signature and address. All defenses and motions should be clearly labeled. Filing the answer takes basically the same steps as the complaint, except that there is no summons. One must attach a certificate of service to the answer and mail a copy to all parties.

Under the Federal Rules of Civil Procedure, a defendant has 20 days from service of complaint and summons to file an answer. The prescribed period for filing an answer may be different in your state court, so check your state rules of procedure carefully.

When a defendant wants to assert a claim against the plaintiff, the defendant files a counterclaim. A counterclaim is essentially in the form of a complaint in which the defendant takes the role of plaintiff and the original plaintiff takes the role of defendant. The counterclaim must be filed within the time prescribed for filing the answer, subject to certain exceptions in FRCivP 13(e). The plaintiff then files a responsive pleading to the counterclaim, termed a reply.

There are two types of counterclaims—permissive and compulsory. A compulsory counterclaim must be asserted, or else the defendant loses the right to assert the claim in a separate lawsuit. FRCivP 13(a) provides that a counterclaim is compulsory when the claim arises out of the transaction or occurrence that is the subject matter of the opposing party's claim and the claim does not require the presence of parties over whom the court cannot acquire jurisdiction. A permissive counterclaim involves a claim that need not be brought as part of the original lawsuit. It concerns claims that do not arise out of the same transaction or occurrence as the original claim. Study the Smith v. Jones and Green example in the text to apply these terms.

A cross-claim is a pleading that states a claim by one party against another party—for example, a claim by one defendant against another defendant. If a defendant filed a counterclaim against two coplaintiffs, a plaintiff could file a cross-claim against the other coplaintiff. FRCivP 13(g) requires that the cross-claim arise out of the same transaction or occurrence that is the subject matter either of the original action or of the counterclaim, or relating to any property that is the subject matter of the original action. A cross-claim may be contingent; that is, a party may assert that if he is liable for all or part of the claim, then the coparty is liable to him. Cross-claims must be filed within the time prescribed for filing an answer.

The format of counterclaims and cross-claims is similar to that of complaints. See the examples in the text. If the defendant requests a jury trial in a counterclaim, that request should be stated conspicuously.

Impleader or third-party practice involves bringing additional parties into the lawsuit and is governed by FRCivP 14(a). This is different from counterclaims and cross-claims, which involve the original parties to the lawsuit. Study the Smith v. Jones and Green example, in which Robertson is brought in as a third-party defendant. When a defendant files a third-party complaint, the defendant is denominated the "defendant and third-party plaintiff." Unless the third-party complaint is filed within 10 days after serving the original answer, court permission is required to file the third-party complaint.

The third-party complaint must be accompanied by a summons and served on the third-party defendant in accordance with the service-of-process requirements of FRCivP 4. Copies must be mailed to all other parties, together with a certificate of service, in the usual manner prescribed in FRCivP 5 for pleadings subsequent to the complaint. Other parties may contest impleader and move the court to strike the third-party claim or to sever it and hear it in a separate trial. FRCivP 14(a) allows a third-party defendant to assert defenses in an answer and/or Rule 12 motions, and to file a counterclaim.

FRCivP 15 allows parties to amend pleadings, and permission to amend is granted liberally. A party may amend a pleading once as a matter of right when no responsive pleading has yet been filed. If no responsive pleading is permitted (for example, a reply to a counterclaim), a party may amend the pleading within 20 days of service, if the action has not been placed on a trial calendar.

Otherwise, court permission is required unless opposing counsel consents to the amendment, in which case a stipulation or consent order may be filed. When a motion to amend is required, the motion must state explicitly the reasons for the amendment and the proposed amended language. In fact, the amended pleading is usually attached as an exhibit to the motion to amend. The adverse party may file a motion opposing the motion to amend. Motions to amend are freely granted unless they would result in undue prejudice to the opposing party.

Removal is the transfer of a lawsuit from a state court to a federal court. Only a defendant may seek removal. A case is removable to federal court only if there is a basis for federal jurisdiction—federal question, diversity, or the like. The federal jurisdiction basis must exist at the time the notice of removal is filed. Thus, if a complaint states no claim on which federal jurisdiction may be based, but the amended complaint adds information on which federal jurisdiction may be based, a notice of removal may be filed after the amended complaint. Every defendant must agree to removal.

The removal procedure is explained by 28 U.S.C. §1446(a). The defendant seeking removal files a notice of removal in the United States district court for the district in which the state court action is pending. The notice of removal must state the grounds for removal, together with a copy of all process, pleadings, and orders served on the defendant in the action. As we noted, the basis for removal may be federal question or diversity jurisdiction. There are also specific federal statutes allowing removal in certain types of lawsuits, such as civil rights actions. The text contains other examples.

The rules for deadlines for filing notice of removal require special attention and are set forth in 28 U.S.C. §1146(b). There are three basic rules. First, when the initial pleading (usually the complaint) contains a basis for removal, the defendant must file the notice of removal within 30 days of receiving the complaint, or within 30 days of receiving the summons when the summons is served without the complaint, whichever period is shorter. The second rule applies when the basis for removal first appears in an amended pleading. In this instance, the notice of removal may be filed within 30 days after receipt by the defendant of an amended pleading, motion, order, or other paper from which it may first be ascertained that the case is one that is or has become removable. The third rule applies when the basis for federal jurisdiction is diversity of citizenship. When diversity arises after the initial pleading, the notice of removal must be filed within one year after the commencement of the action in state court.

When an action is removed to federal court, it does not necessarily stay there for the course of the litigation. The action may be remanded back to state court at any time before final judgment when it appears that the district court lacks subject matter jurisdiction. For instance, complete diversity may be destroyed if a defendant is added who is a citizen of the same state as the plaintiff.

Rules for removal appear in 28 U.S.C. §§1441–1450 and should be studied carefully when a complex removal question arises. Note that 28 U.S.C. §1445 states certain types of actions that cannot be removed from state court.

Chapter 7 Subsequent Pleadings

STUDY QUESTIONS

1. Describe the steps you must take to inform the parties to a lawsuit that a third-party complaint has been filed.

2. May a motion to amend a complaint be filed after the answer and all other responsive pleadings are filed?

3. How may a party obtain an extension of time to file a response to a pleading or motion?

4. Name the seven grounds for a motion to dismiss pursuant to FRCivP 12(b). Which of these grounds can usually be cured and which cannot?

5. Explain under what circumstances a motion for more definite statement should be filed.

6. Explain the alternatives a defendant has in responding to each allegation in the complaint.

7. Explain the meaning of "affirmative defense."

8. List some commonly asserted affirmative defenses.

9. How does the filing of a Rule 12 motion affect the time limit for filing an answer?

10. Define the term "counterclaim" and explain the difference between a compulsory counterclaim and a permissive counterclaim.

11. Explain the rule stated in FRCivP 13(g) as to what type of claim may be asserted in a cross-claim.

12. Explain the nature and purpose of a third-party complaint.

13. How is impleader different from counterclaims and cross-claims?

14. Explain when a third-party plaintiff must obtain leave of court to file a third-party complaint.

15. When does a party need leave of court to file an amended complaint?

16. Discuss the grounds on which a notice of removal may be based.

17. Explain the rules governing deadlines for filing notices of removal.

TEST YOUR KNOWLEDGE

MULTIPLE CHOICE

1. A third-party defendant is allowed to file

    a. an answer.
    b. a Rule 12 motion to dismiss.
    c. a counterclaim against another third-party defendant.
    d. All of the above
    e. a and b only

2. A motion to amend a complaint should be accompanied by

    a. a notice of motion.
    b. a copy of the proposed amended complaint.
    c. a certificate of service.
    d. b and c only
    e. All of the above

3. An extension of time to file a response may be granted

    a. at any stage in the litigation for any reason.
    b. for good cause, when the extension is requested before the prescribed period ends.
    c. for good cause, when the extension is requested after the prescribed period ends.
    d. All of the above

4. A motion aimed at deleting scandalous, prejudicial language from a pleading is a

    a. motion to amend.
    b. motion to dismiss for failure to state a claim upon which relief can be granted.
    c. motion to strike.
    d. motion to dismiss for lack of subject matter jurisdiction.

5. When the defendant is the United States or an officer or agency of the U.S. government, the defendant is allowed _____ days to file an answer or other responsive pleading.

    a. 20
    b. 30
    c. 10
    d. 60

6. An answer may contain all of the following except

    a. a cross-claim.
    b. a counterclaim
    c. A third-party complaint.
    d. Affirmative defenses.

7. A response to a counterclaim is called a

   a. reply.
   b. cross-claim.
   c. affirmative defense.
   d. answer.

8. The format of a counterclaim is most like a

   a. answer.
   b. complaint.
   c. motion to dismiss.
   d. amended complaint.

9. The transfer of a lawsuit from state court to federal court is called

   a. dismissal.
   b. removal.
   c. impleader.
   d. third-party practice.

10. The jurisdictional basis on which removal is based may appear in

   a. the original complaint.
   b. the answer.
   c. the amended complaint.
   d. All of the above
   e. a and c only

TRUE/FALSE

1. T F   In a permissive counterclaim, a party need not assert the jurisdictional basis of the claim.

2. T F   If a motion to dismiss for improper venue is not included in a motion to strike or an answer, the defendant can lose the right to assert this defense later.

3. T F   A motion to strike should be filed before filing an answer.

4. T F   A motion for more definite statement should be filed after filing an answer.

5. T F   If in the answer a defendant does not deny an allegation of the complaint, the allegation is deemed to be denied.

6. T F   A defendant may not request a jury trial in its answer.

7. T F   When a party receives by mail a notice that she is required to respond, 10 days are added to the prescribed period for response.

8. T F   A motion to dismiss under FRCivP 12(b)(6) may not be overcome by amending the complaint.

9. T F   A Rule 12 motion may be filed separately or as part of an answer.

10. T F Some Rule 12 motions are deemed waived if not included with a motion to strike or an answer.

11. T F A motion for a more definite statement should be filed any time the pleadings do not cover a fact you need to know.

12. T F The general rule under the Federal Rules of Civil Procedure is that a defendant has 30 days from date of service of the complaint to file an answer.

13. T F A compulsory counterclaim requires an assertion of a jurisdictional basis independent from the original complaint.

14. T F When a codefendant files an answer and/or counterclaim, the codefendant need not specify whether the pleadings are filed by that codefendant alone or in conjunction with other codefendants.

15. T F Court permission is never necessary to file a third-party complaint.

16. T F Once a lawsuit has been removed to federal court, it may be remanded to state court under some circumstances.

17. T F Federal jurisdiction need not exist at the time a notice of removal is filed, provided that there is a possibility that a jurisdictional ground may arise later.

18. T F After a lawsuit is removed to federal court, the state court retains jurisdiction over some procedural matters.

Chapter 7   Subsequent Pleadings

ANSWERS TO STUDY QUESTIONS

1. The third-party defendant must be served with the third-party complaint and third-party summons in accordance with FRCivP 4. All other parties are mailed copies in accordance with FRCivP 5.

2. Yes. FRCivP 5 allows amendments to pleadings even after responsive pleadings are filed, so long as the case is not yet on a trial calendar and it would not be too prejudicial to the other parties.

3. Usually the attorney/paralegal team first contacts counsel for the opposing party to see whether they will consent to an extension of time. If the opposing party's counsel consents, the parties file a stipulation of extension or consent order stating the agreed-upon extension. If the opposing party will not agree to an extension, the party must seek the court's permission for an extension. FRCivP 6(b) provides that if the extension is requested before expiration of the time originally allowed for response, the moving party must establish "good cause" for granting an extension. If the request is made after expiration of the prescribed period, the moving party must prove that the failure to file a timely response was due to "excusable neglect."

4. The seven grounds for dismissal pursuant to FRCivP 12(b) are:
   12(b)(1) Lack of jurisdiction over the subject matter
   12(b)(2) Lack of jurisdiction over the person
   12(b)(3) Improper venue
   12(b)(4) Insufficiency of process
   12(b)(5) Insufficiency of service of process
   12(b)(6) Failure to state a claim upon which relief can be granted
   12(b)(7) Failure to join a party under Rule 19.

   Lack of subject matter jurisdiction cannot be cured. If you have filed suit in a court that does not have jurisdiction, the case can be dismissed. Lack of personal jurisdiction cannot always be cured. This usually concerns whether a long-arm statute applies or minimum contacts exist. The outcome depends on the court's decision as to whether personal jurisdiction can be asserted.

   Deficiencies related to service of process can usually be cured by serving process again, this time correctly. Improper venue is usually not a fatal flaw, because most courts will transfer the action to a court in the proper district rather than dismiss the action outright. Failure to state a claim upon which relief can be granted can usually be cured with an amended complaint. A Rule 12(b)(7) motion is usually not fatal if one can find and obtain jurisdiction over the party.

5. FRCivP 12(e) provides that if a pleading is so vague or ambiguous that a party cannot frame a responsive pleading, then a motion for more definite statement may be filed before filing a responsive pleading. Before filing a motion for more definite statement, one should review the pleadings, bearing in mind that FRCivP 8 requires only a short and plain statement of the facts. A motion for more definite statement need not be filed if you have questions about facts that may be ascertained through the discovery process, but only if the allegations are so vague or confusing that you cannot formulate a response.

6. The defendant may either admit or deny each allegation. A paragraph in the complaint may be admitted in part and denied in part. Defendants may also state that they are without sufficient knowledge or information to form a belief as to the truth of an averment, and this is considered a denial.

7. An affirmative defense is a defense that goes beyond denying the allegations in the complaint. Rather, it brings out a new matter that serves as a defense, even if the allegations in the complaint are true. A common example is the statute of limitations defense, which means that the plaintiff is barred from filing the lawsuit because the claim was not asserted within the time allowed by statute. FRCivP 8(c) sets forth numerous types of affirmative defenses.

8. Some common affirmative defenses are statute of limitations, contributory negligence, assumption of risk, discharge in bankruptcy, fraud, release, res judicata, and waiver. FRCivP 8(c) also allows as an affirmative defense "any other matter constituting an avoidance or affirmative defense."

9. If the court denies the Rule 12 motion, the defendant has 10 days after notice of the court's decision to file an answer. When a court grants a motion for a more definite statement, the plaintiff files an amended complaint, and the defendant must respond within 10 days of service of the more definite statement.

10. A counterclaim is a pleading in which a defendant asserts a claim against a plaintiff. A compulsory counterclaim involves a claim that arises out of the same transaction or occurrence that is the subject matter of the opposing party's claim. A compulsory counterclaim must be asserted in the original lawsuit and may not be the subject of a separate lawsuit. A permissive counterclaim involves a claim that does not arise out of the same transaction or occurrence. It need not be asserted as part of the original lawsuit, and if a permissive counterclaim makes the litigation too complex, the court may order it severed. In contrast to a compulsory counterclaim, a permissive counterclaim requires assertion of its own jurisdictional basis, separate from the original complaint.

11. A claim asserted by one coparty against another coparty in a cross-claim must arise out of the same transaction or occurrence that is the subject of the original complaint or out of a counterclaim that is part of the original action. A cross-claim may also relate to any property that is the subject matter of the original answer.

12. The purpose of a third-party complaint (impleader) is to assert that a person not already a party to the action may be liable to the defendant (third-party plaintiff) for all or part of the original plaintiff's claim against the defendant.

13. Impleader brings in persons not already parties to the lawsuit. A counterclaim is a claim by an original defendant against an original plaintiff. A cross-claim is a claim by one coparty to the original lawsuit against another coparty.

14. A third-party plaintiff may file a third-party complaint without the court's permission if the third-party complaint is filed within 10 days after serving the original answer. Otherwise, the third-party plaintiff must file a motion requesting court permission to file the third-party complaint.

15. A party may amend a pleading once as a matter of right when no responsive pleading has been filed and the action has not been placed on a trial calendar. If counsel for the opposing party consents, the parties may simply file a stipulation or consent order stating their agreement to the amendment. Otherwise, a party needs the court's permission to file an amended complaint.

16. A ground for federal jurisdiction must exist before a lawsuit may be transferred from state court to federal court. The ground may be federal question jurisdiction or diversity jurisdiction. In addition, several federal statutes specifically provide that removal is allowed in certain types of actions. These statutes include U.S.C. §§1441–1444, and apply to civil actions against foreign states, civil rights actions, foreclosure against the United States, and actions involving federal officers of members of the armed forces.

17. When the basis for removal is stated in the initial pleading, usually the complaint, the notice of removal must be filed within 30 days of receiving the complaint, or within 30 days of receiving the summons when the summons is served without the complaint, whichever period is shorter. When the basis for removal first appears in an amended pleading, the notice of removal must be filed within 30 days of the amended pleading, motion, order, or other paper from which it may first be ascertained that the case is one that is or has become removable. When the basis for federal jurisdiction is diversity of citizenship of the parties, the notice of removal must be filed within one year after the commencement of the action in state court.

ANSWERS TO TEST YOUR KNOWLEDGE

MULTIPLE CHOICE

1. e	6. c
2. e	7. a
3. c	8. b
4. c	9. b
5. d	10. e

TRUE/FALSE

1. F	7. F	13. F
2. T	8. F	14. F
3. T	9. T	15. F
4. T	10. T	16. T
5. F	11. F	17. F
6. F	12. F	18. F

8 MOTION PRACTICE AND MOTIONS FOR ENTRY OF JUDGMENT WITHOUT TRIAL

SUMMARY

The first major topic in Chapter 8 is motion practice. A motion is an application to a court for an order directing an act in favor of the applicant. Numerous motions are made throughout the course of a lawsuit, ranging from extensions of time to file a response to summary judgment, requesting the court to enter judgment without the necessity of a trial.

FRCivP 7(b) sets forth three requirements for the form of motions. First, a motion must be in writing unless made orally during a hearing or trial. Second, the motion must "state with particularity the grounds" on which it is based. Third, the motion must "set forth the relief or order sought."

The format for motions is the same as for pleadings. A motion has a caption that includes the name of the court, names of the parties, and file number. The title of the motion itself should be stated specifically—for example, "Motion for Judgment on the Pleadings." As with a pleading, the body of the motion is arranged in numbered paragraphs, and the motion is signed by the attorney and contains the attorney's address and phone number. In accordance with FRCivP 7(b), the grounds that justify granting the motion must be stated specifically.

A notice of motion accompanies the motion itself, stating the time and location of the hearing on the motion. FRCivP 6(d) requires that the motion, all supporting documents, and notice of motion must be served on all parties to the litigation not later than five days before the date set for the hearing.

Supporting documents accompany many motions, particularly the more complex motions such as summary judgment. Affidavits, statements signed under oath explaining the pertinent facts, are often attached. Documents on which the litigation is based (e.g., contracts) may also be attached as exhibits.

Often a memorandum of law is submitted, explaining the pertinent law and applying the law to the facts of the case to justify why the motion should be granted. Local court rules may address such specifics as page limitations and format.

The motion, notice of motion, and all supporting documents must be served on all the parties. The general rule is that these be served at least five days before the hearing, but there are exceptions; motions for summary judgment, for example, must be filed at least ten days before the hearing.

It is crucial to respond to all motions. Many courts deem a motion unopposed if no response is filed. A memorandum of law should be submitted in response to the other party's memorandum. If the parties agree that a motion should be granted, they may submit a consent order, which states the parties' consent to the relief requested. Judges are not required to sign consent orders, but they usually do. All responsive motions, with supporting documents, must be served on all parties.

Hearings on motions are often held to allow the attorneys to argue to the judge why their motion should be granted or why they oppose the other party's motion. The hearings are sometimes scheduled by the court and sometimes by the attorneys. Paralegals who assist in scheduling the hearing should, if possible, check with opposing counsel to see if they are available for the chosen time. Oral argument is not held for some simple motions, and it may be waived by counsel even for a complex motion. However, where the issues are complex and many documents must be considered, a hearing is usually held.

After judges decide whether to grant or deny a motion, they enter an order stating their decision. The order may simply state whether the motion is granted or denied, or the court may publish a lengthy explanation, depending upon the nature of the motion. Some courts require the attorneys to submit a proposed order when filing a motion. A proposed order is the order that the moving party would like the judge to sign, granting the relief requested. Even if a proposed order is not required, it is wise to submit one to express why your client should receive the relief requested. This is an opportunity to influence the judge with a clear argument.

The next major topic is default judgment. When a party fails to plead a defense to a claim within the allotted time, the party asserting the claim may move for default judgment. This is a fairly simple procedure that begins with the filing of a Request to Enter Default. Entry of Default is signed by the clerk of court and indicates that the party, usually the defendant, has not responded within the allotted time. If the amount in controversy is a sum certain or a sum that can readily be ascertained, then the moving party files a motion for the clerk of court to enter a default judgment. If the amount in controversy is not a sum certain or cannot readily be ascertained, then only a judge can enter the default judgment, and a hearing may be necessary to determine the amount. After entry of default, it is possible for the defending party to move to set aside the entry of default and avoid the default judgment. Even after a default judgment has been entered, a party can move to set aside the actual judgment. The moving party must establish ''good cause'' for setting aside the default judgment, and the motion must be filed within one year from the date of judgment.

Default judgment is not limited to defendants that fail to respond. It may also be entered against a third-party defendant, a codefendant in the case of a cross-claim, or a plaintiff in the case of a counterclaim. Study Figures 8-7 and 8-8 through 8-14 in the text to understand the procedure for obtaining and attacking a default judgment. Remember that entry of default and default judgment are not the same thing.

The next major section addresses judgment on the pleadings, which is governed by FRCivP 12(c). This motion may be filed after the pleadings are closed but not so late in the litigation as to interfere with the trial. The court must look only at the pleadings in making a determination whether judgment on the pleadings should be granted. The court must consider the pleadings in the light most favorable to the nonmoving party. To prevail on a motion for judgment on the pleadings, the plaintiff must establish that the defendant's pleadings raise no valid defense to the plaintiff's claim. The defendant must show that the allegations in the plaintiff's complaint would not allow any recovery. This determination usually turns on questions of law, not factual disputes. A common example is when a plaintiff files a complaint after the statute of limitations has expired. If material facts are in dispute, judgment on the pleadings is usually not proper. A material fact is one that affects the outcome of the case.

Because pleadings rarely show that one party has no chance of prevailing, motions for judgment on the pleadings are rarely granted. There is a strong policy of allowing parties the opportunity to prove their case at trial. If the court looks beyond the face of the pleadings, a motion for judgment on the pleadings is automatically converted to a motion for summary judgment.

Motions for summary judgment are commonly filed dispositive motions. FRCivP 56(c) provides the standard the court must apply in deciding a motion for summary judgment. It states that summary judgment is proper when there is no genuine issue as to any material fact and the moving party is entitled to a judgment as a matter of law. The court considers the pleadings, discovery materials such as answers to interrogatories and depositions, admissions on file, and affidavits submitted by the parties. The determination is based on the undisputed, material facts. Parties also file memoranda of law explaining why summary judgment should be granted.

A party may also move for partial summary judgment, when the party claims to be entitled to summary judgment on some, but not all, issues. This is common where a party admits liability but does not agree on the amount of damages.

Motions for summary judgment may be filed for counterclaims and cross-claims, as well as for claims asserted in the complaint. As to timing, a party against whom a claim is asserted may move for summary judgment at any time. A party asserting a claim (i.e., a plaintiff) cannot file for summary judgment until 20 days have elapsed from the commencement of the action. Both parties may move for summary judgment, resulting in what is known as cross-motions for summary judgment.

The actual motion for summary judgment is usually quite brief. (Revisit Figures 8-17 and 8-19 in the text.) The supporting documents, however, may be voluminous; among them may be affidavits explaining the facts that justify summary judgment. Pursuant to FRCivP 56(e)-(g), the affidavits must be based on personal knowledge and must show that the affiant is competent to testify to the matters stated. In addition, the facts stated in the affidavit must be admissible in evidence. A party that asserts a motion for summary judgment in bad faith may be ordered to pay to the other party the costs involved in responding to the motion, including attorney's fees. A party opposing summary judgment must establish specific facts showing that there is a genuine issue for trial.

The memoranda of law supporting motions for summary judgment may be lengthy; they set forth the facts that are undisputed and document how the law supports the party's position. As with other motions, the opposing party must respond and file a reply memorandum of law explaining why the motion should not be granted. Oral argument is often held, and notice of the hearing must be served on the opposing parties at least ten days before the hearing. Even if a motion for summary judgment is denied, the extensive preparation in connection with the motion will help the parties prepare for trial.

Chapter 8   Motion Practice and Motions for Entry of Judgment Without Trial

STUDY QUESTIONS

1. What are the three principal motions for entry of judgment without trial?

2. Explain how motions regulate the course of the litigation.

3. Explain how the format of motions is like or unlike the format for pleadings.

4. Explain the purpose of the notice of motion and the deadlines for filing a notice of motion.

5. Explain the types of documents that may be submitted in support of motions.

6. Explain what an affidavit is and why it is considered more reliable than some statements.

7. On whom must the motion be served? Must all supporting documents be served as well?

8. What should a party do when it opposes a motion?

9. When a judge makes a determination concerning the disposition of a motion, an order is entered. Explain what the order generally contains and any guidelines the judge may have in determining the content of the order.

10. Explain the difference between a judgment and an order.

11. When is it appropriate to file a motion for default judgment?

12. Explain the parties, in addition to the defendant, against whom a default judgment may be entered.

13. Explain the documents that must be filed to obtain a default judgment.

14. Explain the grounds for setting aside entry of default or a default judgment.

15. At what point in the litigation is it proper to file a motion for judgment on the pleadings?

16. What may the court consider in deciding a motion for judgment on the pleadings?

17. How must the court view the pleadings and under what circumstances is the motion for judgment on the pleadings generally granted?

18. Why are motions for judgment on the pleadings seldom granted?

19. State the standard a court must apply in deciding a motion for summary judgment.

20. What documents may the court consider in deciding a motion for summary judgment?

21. Explain the circumstances under which partial summary judgment may be proper.

22. What may the court do when a party submits affidavits in bad faith?

23. Why must a party opposed to a motion for summary judgment file a response?

TEST YOUR KNOWLEDGE

MULTIPLE CHOICE

1. Which of the following are requirements for affidavits submitted in support of a motion for summary judgment?

   a. The affidavits must be based on personal knowledge.
   b. The facts in the affidavits must be admissible in evidence.
   c. The affidavits must not be submitted in bad faith.
   d. All of the above

2. Which of the following must be submitted to obtain a default judgment?

   a. Affidavit in compliance with Soldiers' and Sailors' Relief Act
   b. Request for entry of default judgment
   c. Affidavit to prove the amount of the judgment to which the plaintiff is entitled
   d. a and c only
   e. All of the above

3. Which of the following may a court consider in ruling on a motion for summary judgment?

 a. Portions of depositions
 b. Affidavits stating facts that are inadmissible at trial
 c. The pleadings
 d. a and c only
 e. All of the above

4. Which of the following are requirements for motions under the Federal Rules of Civil Procedure?

 a. The motion must set forth the relief sought.
 b. The motion must be in writing unless made orally at trial.
 c. A hearing must be held on the motion.
 d. a and b only
 e. All of the above

5. In a motion for judgment on the pleadings, the court may consider

 a. the pleadings only.
 b. a memorandum of law submitted by the moving party.
 c. portions of depositions.
 d. a and b only
 e. All of the above

6. Which of the following are true about memoranda of law submitted in support of a motion?

 a. The opposing party should also submit a memorandum of law.
 b. The memorandum of law should include a statement of facts.
 c. The memorandum of law should include a discussion of the applicable case law.
 d. a and c only
 e. All of the above

7. A motion for summary judgment should be captioned

 a. "Motion."
 b. "Motion for Summary Judgment."
 c. "Dispositive Motion."
 d. Any of the above would be acceptable.

8. A notice of motion for a hearing on a motion for summary judgment should be served on opposing parties

 a. at least 10 days before the scheduled hearing.
 b. at least 5 days before the scheduled hearing.
 c. within a reasonable time before the scheduled hearing.
 d. None of the above

9. When entering an order disposing of a motion, the court may use

 a. the proposed order submitted by the moving party.
 b. the proposed order submitted by the nonmoving party.
 c. a preprinted court form.
 d. Any of the above

10. Which of these statements is true about *ex parte* motions?

    a. They are usually entered without a hearing.
    b. They are appropriate for many types of motions.
    c. They are appropriate for motions for temporary restraining orders.
    d. a and c only
    e. All of the above

TRUE/FALSE

1. T (F)   Even if the parties agree on a motion, a hearing must be held.

2. (T) F   A judgment may be entered without having a trial.

3. T (F)   A motion must stand on its own merits and may not be supported by other documents.

4. T F   A default judgment may be entered against a codefendant who does not file a timely response to a cross-claim.

5. T (F)   Once a default judgment is entered, it cannot be attacked by subsequent motions.

6. T (F)   In deciding a motion for judgment on the pleadings, the court must view the allegations of the opposing party as false.

7. (T) F   A party that opposes a motion for summary judgment must establish that there is a genuine issue for trial.

8. T (F)   The Federal Rules of Civil Procedure do not allow amendments of pleadings in order to cure a defect in pleadings that would otherwise justify judgment on the pleadings.

9. T (F)   The court will not consider a motion for summary judgment unless it is supported by a memorandum of law.

10. T (F)   A response must be filed only to complex motions such as judgments on the pleadings.

11. T (F)   A party opposing a motion for summary judgment may rely on the pleadings as its response to the motion.

12. (T) F   A default judgment may be appropriate even when the amount of the damages may not readily be ascertained.

13. T (F)   Unlike pleadings, motions need not be signed by the attorney of record.

14. (T) F   Local rules of court may require that a proposed order be submitted with a motion.

15. T (F)   Judicial opinions explaining why a motion was granted are always published.

Chapter 8 Motion Practice and Motions for Entry of Judgment Without Trial

ANSWERS TO STUDY QUESTIONS

1. They are motion for default judgment, motion for judgment on the pleadings, and motion for summary judgment.

2. Motions are filed throughout the course of the litigation. They often pertain to procedural matters, such as a motion for an extension to file a response. Dispositive motions are more substantive and can end the litigation before a trial is held. Some motions are made orally at trial, such as motions regarding the admissibility of evidence.

3. The format for motions is for the most part like pleadings. The motion has a caption that includes the name of the court, title of the action (names of parties), and file number. The name of the motion is stated with particularity: for example, ''motion for judgment on the pleadings,'' not simply ''motion.'' Like that of a pleading, the body of a motion consists of numbered paragraphs. And in another likeness to pleadings, motions are signed by the attorneys of record and include their addresses and telephone numbers.

4. The purpose of the notice of motion is to inform the other parties that a motion has been filed and especially to inform them of the date a hearing has been scheduled. With most motions, only a five-day notice before the hearing date is required. With motions for summary judgment, a ten-day notice is required.

5. Documents that are the subject of the litigation, such as contracts, may be attached as exhibits to the motion. Affidavits explaining the facts that justify granting the motion are often attached. A memorandum of law, or brief, is often submitted explaining how the application of the law to the facts of the particular case justifies granting the motion. With some motions, such as summary judgment, portions of discovery materials may be attached in support. The same documents are submitted when a party opposes a motion.

6. An affidavit is a written statement bearing the notarized signature of the person who makes it. Because the affiant must swear that the statement is true before his or her signature may be notarized, affidavits are considered more reliable than regular written or oral statements.

7. The motion, notice of motion, and all supporting documents must be served on all parties to the litigation. Service is generally by mail, and a certificate of service is attached to the motion.

8. The party should file its own motion asking the court to deny the other party's motion and explaining why. The motion in opposition should be supported by documentation just as the motion it opposes. A memorandum of law is usually helpful to explain to the court why the law justifies denying the other party's motion.

9. The judge enters an order stating whether the motion is granted or denied. The judge explains the rationale for the decision. Most parties submit to the judge a proposed order that is in a form ready for signature and explains why the moving party is entitled to the relief sought. Some local court rules require the submission of proposed orders. Even if a proposed order is not mandatory, it is a good idea to submit one because it is in essence a statement of why the relief you seek should be granted. Judges sometimes use preprinted forms for simple motions that they hear often.

10. A judgment states the final disposition of a lawsuit and terminates the litigation. An order resolves only a specific issue or issues, not all the issues. An order shapes the outcome of the litigation but is not the final statement of the outcome.

11. It is appropriate when the party against whom a claim is asserted does not file a defense within the allotted time.

12. In the case of a counterclaim, a default judgment may be entered against a plaintiff. In the case of a cross-claim, a default judgment may be entered against a coparty, such as a codefendant. When a third-party complaint has been filed, default judgment may be entered against the third-party defendant.

13. First the moving party files a Request to Enter Default. Entry of default states that the party has not responded within the allotted time. The Request to Enter Default is accompanied by an affidavit signed by the moving party's attorney, explaining when the complaint was filed, when service of process was completed, and further stating that the party against whom the claim was filed has not responded with a defense.

    The next step is to file the documents necessary to obtain the actual default judgment. When the amount in controversy is a sum certain or a sum that is readily ascertainable, the default judgment may be granted by the clerk of court. Otherwise, a judge is required to enter the default judgment. A Request for Entry of Default Judgment is filed and is accompanied by an affidavit to prove the amount to which the moving party is entitled. One also submits an affidavit in compliance with the Soldiers' and Sailors' Civil Relief Act stating that the adverse parties are not in the military service of the United States. It is the better practice also to submit a proposed judgment for the clerk of court or judge to sign.

14. The grounds are those enumerated in FRCivP 60, which addresses the grounds for attacking judgments in general. Basically, the moving party must establish ''good cause'' for not responding within the allotted time. Good cause may exist when the attorney or client was seriously ill. Good cause is most likely to be established when the motion to set aside is filed as promptly as possible, establishes that the party has a good defense, and explains a valid reason why a response was not timely filed.

15. A motion for judgment on the pleadings may be filed after the pleadings are closed but within such time as not to delay the trial.

16. The court may look only at the face of the pleadings and at nothing beyond the pleadings.

17. The court must consider the pleadings in the light most favorable to the nonmoving party. The court generally considers only the undisputed facts. A plaintiff is usually entitled to judgment on the pleadings when the defendant has raised no valid defense. A defendant is usually entitled to judgment on the pleadings when the plaintiff's complaint would not allow recovery, even when everything stated in the complaint is true.

18. It is very rare for a plaintiff to allege facts that could not possibly support some type of relief. It is equally rare for a defendant to assert nothing that may be a valid defense. In addition, there is a strong policy of allowing parties the opportunity to present their case at trial.

19. FRCivP 56 provides that summary judgment is proper when there is no genuine issue as to any material fact and the moving party is entitled to a judgment as a matter of law.

20. The court may look to the pleadings, affidavits submitted by the parties, pertinent portions of discovery materials, documents (such as contracts) that are the subject of the litigation, and admissions on file. The court will also read and consider the memoranda of law submitted by the parties in support of or in opposition to the motion.

21. Partial summary judgment may be proper when a party is entitled to judgment on some, but not all, issues in the lawsuit. A common example is when a party admits liability, but there remains a dispute as to the amount of damages.

22. FRCivP 56(g) states that the court may order the party that submitted the affidavits to pay to the party forced to respond the expenses of preparing the response, including attorney's fees.

23. FRCivP 56(e) specifically states that a party opposing a motion for summary judgment must file affidavits in response and may not rely on the pleadings alone.

ANSWERS TO TEST YOUR KNOWLEDGE

MULTIPLE CHOICE

1. d	6. e
2. e	7. b
3. d	8. a
4. d	9. d
5. d	10. d

TRUE/FALSE

1. F	6. F	11. F
2. T	7. T	12. T
3. F	8. F	13. F
4. T	9. F	14. T
5. F	10. F	15. F

9 DISCOVERY

SUMMARY

Discovery is an important topic for paralegals, because much of your work is done in the discovery phase of litigation. Discovery refers to the pretrial methods used by the parties to obtain information from one another. Discovery has several purposes, including clarification of facts and preservation of testimony for later use. One of the primary purposes of discovery is to avoid surprise at trial.

METHODS OF DISCOVERY

There are five principal methods of discovery. One is the deposition, where an attorney orally questions a witness, who responds under oath. A court reporter records the testimony and prepares a transcript. A second method is the use of the interrogatories, written questions submitted by one party to another and answered "separately and fully in writing under oath," unless a valid objection is raised. A third method is requests for production of documents and things and for entry upon land for inspection. Of the three types of requests that this allows, requests for production of documents are the most common. Parties may also request things—that is, tangible objects—for inspection, and may request entry upon land to inspect, survey, or otherwise investigate the property. A fourth method is requests for admission. These are written requests asking other parties to admit that certain things are true. If a party admits the truth of a fact, that fact is deemed to be true throughout the entire lawsuit. The fifth method of discovery is through physical or mental examination of a person whose condition is at issue in the lawsuit.

RULES THAT GOVERN THE DISCOVERY PROCESS

The rules that govern the discovery process derive from the same source as other rules for civil litigation—Federal Rules of Civil Procedure, state rules of civil procedure in state court, and local court rules. State rules tend to follow federal rules, but there can be important differences. FRCivP 26-37 govern discovery, and you should know them all. Consult local court rules regularly, as they often contain important requirements.

An example of how rules can vary is seen in rules regarding whether to file discovery materials with the court. FRCivP 5(d) gives the court the option, whereas some state rules specifically direct parties not to file discovery documents, and other state and/or local rules leave the filing to the judge's discretion.

SEQUENCE AND TIMING OF DISCOVERY

FRCivP 26 allows parties to use discovery methods in any sequence, unless the judge directs otherwise. One common sequence is to use interrogatories first, followed by depositions when you have identified the other party's witnesses through interrogatories. Requests for admission follow, after the facts and issues have been sufficiently narrowed. Physical and mental examinations may follow in personal injury cases. Different types of lawsuits may require different sequences.

The timing is usually left to the parties without court intervention. However, there are deadlines for responding to interrogatories and other requests, and the consequences of missing a deadline can be severe. Local rules may impose deadlines for completion of all discovery; judges may also set deadlines, especially if the parties abuse discovery.

DUTY TO SUPPLEMENT RESPONSES

Parties must update and supplement their answers when a prior response is no longer accuate. The duty to supplement continues throughout the litigation.

SCOPE OF DISCOVERY

The general rule for scope of discovery is in FRCivP 26(b)(1), which allows discovery of any matter that is relevant, is not privileged, and is reasonably calculated to lead to admissible evidence. Note that the evidence itself does not have to be admissible. For example, hearsay evidence that fits no exception to the hearsay rule can lead to admissible evidence. FRCivP 26 specifically allows the discovery of insurance agreements that may serve to pay the judgment.

SPECIAL RULES CONCERNING EXPERT WITNESSES

For the purpose of discovery, we consider expert witnesses as belonging in one of two groups. Those who are expected to testify at trial are subject to discovery as to their identities, the subject matter on which they are expected to testify, the substance of the facts and opinions about which they will testify, and a summary of the grounds for their opinions. The knowledge and opinions of the second group, experts who are not expected to testify at trial, are generally not discoverable unless exceptional circumstances make it impracticable to obtain facts or opinons on a given subject by any other means.

LIMITATIONS ON DISCOVERY

Some information is protected from discovery, and paralegals must remain alert for privileged material so that it will not be inadvertently disclosed. Two common privileges to watch for are attorney-client privilege and work product privilege. While attorney-client privilege is self-explanatory, work product privilege (which refers to certain trial preparation materials) demands careful scrutiny. The work product privilege protects the mental impressions, conclusions, opinions, or legal theories of an attorney or other representative of a party concerning the litigation according to FRCivP 26(b)(3). Other trial preparation materials may be discoverable if the other party is unable without undue hardship to obtain the substantial equivalent of the materials by other means.

Parties may obtain protective orders from the court to protect confidential information, such as trade secrets. Parties can also seek protective orders when disclosure would cause annoyance, embarrassment, oppression, or undue burden or expense. FRCivP 26(c) enumerates a number of means of protections from sealing documents to file with the court to limiting the attendance of persons at depositions.

DISCOVERY PLANNING

Planning is important. First review all the facts you have to establish. Then list the possible sources of information. Next, consider the method that is best for obtaining that information. It is important to consider your client's budget, because discovery can be expensive.

INTERROGATORIES

FRCivP 33 addresses the procedure for interrogatories. Only parties to the lawsuit can be required to answer interrogatories. If a party is a corporation, the corporation must appoint an officer or agent to provide answers. Interrogatories may be served on the plaintiff at any time and on the other parties at any time after service of the summons and complaint. A party has 30 days to answer, unless the interrogatories were served concurrently with the summons and complaint, in which case 45 days are allowed. A party must either answer or object to each interrogatory.

Paralegals often draft interrogatories. Sources of questions to include are other files in your office, form books, and records on appeal from similar cases. However, you must always be careful to tailor the questions to your case. This is especially important because most courts limit the number of interrogatories a party can send. Frequent topics include the following: identity of the person answering the interrogatories, whether a corporate defendant has been correctly named in the pleadings, identity of witnesses, information about expert witnesses, information about pertinent documents, details of the other parties' version of the facts, further specification of the amount and type of damages, and insurance coverage. General guidelines in composing interrogatories include making the questions clear, trying to avoid questions that require yes/no answers, and asking the respondent to specify the source of each reply so that you can tell whether that person has first- or second-hand knowledge of the information given. The format for interrogatories includes a caption, introduction with definitions, numbered paragraphs with subparts, attorney signature and address, and certificate of service.

To draft answers to interrogatories, you begin by obtaining the basic information from your clients. Send the clients a copy of the interrogatories, answer any questions they have, and follow up to be sure they return the information in time to prepare the answers. Remember to answer or object to each question. Be especially careful not to disclose confidential information. Besides privilege, grounds for objection may be that the information sought is unreasonably cumulative or duplicative, or the discovery is unduly burdensome and expensive. These are the general grounds for objections for discovery.

The final draft of the answers must be reviewed by the attorney and signed by the attorney and/or client, depending largely on local rules. When the client is a business organization, the company designates someone with sufficient knowledge to answer the interrogatories, and that person signs the responses. The client may be required to sign a statement verifying that the answers are true.

REQUESTS FOR PRODUCTION OF DOCUMENTS AND THINGS

Parties can request that tangible objects be handed over for inspection. A good example is the electric blanket in the Wesser case. Parties may request to enter a person's land to inspect, measure, or survey the property. Documents, the most frequently requested items, include drawings, charts, photographs, and other items specified in FRCivP 34. When items are requested, it is not a valid excuse to say that they are in someone else's possession. The items must be obtained and produced, unless there is a valid reason to object.

Our discussion centers on requests for production of documents, because paralegals frequently play a major role in producing documents. Requests may be served on the plaintiff at any time and on other parties with service of the summons and complaint or at any time afterward. Parties have 30 days to serve answers unless the requests were served with the summons and complaint, in which case they are allowed 45 days.

The format of a request consists of caption, introductory paragraph with definitions if necessary, numbered list of documents requested, attorney signature, and certificate of service. The request should specify the date, time, and location for inspecting or copying the documents. The requests must be clear enough for parties to determine which documents you seek. A request that is unjustifiably broad can be too burdensome or otherwise objectionable.

In large lawsuits production of documents is a massive undertaking. Paralegals may supervise a team of clerical assistants who help to gather and copy the documents. You may have to go through clients' files at their offices or warehouse. Sometimes the clients' own employees search their files for the pertinent information, but you are more likely to get all the needed information if you and your team do the search.

It is important for the attorney/paralegal team to screen the documents to ensure that protected information is not released to the other party. You should focus your review on four categories of information: irrelevant documents, unresponsive documents, confidential documents, and privileged information.

The next big step is to organize the documents for copying. Arrange the documents in a logical order—for example, by subject matter. Assign a number to each document to identify it. These so-called production numbers serve several purposes including forming the basis for an index. The numbers also help you ensure that all documents are accounted for before trial. You are ready to copy the documents. Put them in boxes, labeled on the outside, and make sure that you have enough clerical help for copying and putting the documents back in order.

DEPOSITIONS

There are two types of depositions, written and oral. The most common by far is oral, where an attorney asks the deponent questions, and a court reporter records the questions and answers. After the deposition is over, the court reporter prepares a transcript, which the deponent reviews and corrects, if necessary. Usually the attorney for each party gets a copy of the transcript. Attorneys may use exhibits as part of the questioning, asking a deponent to identify documents and verify signatures. The exhibits are numbered and attached to the transcript.

Both parties and nonparties may be deposed. Deponents may be forced to attend by service of a subpoena. Attorneys generally depose other parties' witnesses rather than their own, because they know what their witnesses are going to say. However, if the attorneys fear that a witness may be unavailable for trial, they may depose the witness to preserve the testimony and introduce it at trial.

A written notice of the deposition is sent to the deponent and the attorneys for all parties. FRCivP 30(b) requires only ''reasonable notice,'' but local rules may require a specific time. (Examine the notice in Figure 9-4 in the text.) The notice states the place, date and time for the deposition. For a nonparty witness, prepare a subpoena (illustrated in text Figure 9-5). The subpoena must be personally served on the witness. When the deponent is a corporation or agency, the notice or subpoena must describe ''with reasonable particularity'' the matters on which examination is sought. The agency or corporation then designates one or more persons to testify.

Depositions are usually held in conference rooms in law offices. The persons present include the deponent, the attorneys for all parties, the court reporter, and often paralegals on the attorneys' teams. The attorney who scheduled the deposition examines the deponent; then there is an opportunity for cross-examination. An attorney may object to a question, but the deponent has to go ahead and answer. Questions of admissibility of the testimony are determined at trial.

After the transcript is reviewed and signed, local rules differ as to the procedure. Some rules direct that the transcript be filed with the court, and others direct that the transcript be delivered to the attorney who took the deposition. Copies go to all attorneys.

Paralegals help arrange depositions by helping to arrange the time and place, making reservations for conference rooms when necessary, arranging for the court reporter, and arranging exhibits to be used in the deposition. During the deposition paralegals may help the attorneys keep track of exhibits, take notes about the testimony, and observe the deponent's demeanor. Be alert for any contradictory statements that the deponent makes.

After a transcript is received, the paralegal often prepares a digest (summary) of the testimony. There are three principal types of digests. One is the witness digest, a simple summary of the testimony in the order it was given. Another is the subject matter index, where a subject appears in the left-hand column and each reference to that subject appears in the right-hand column, with the page number on which the statement appears. The third type of digest is chronological, set up like the subject matter digest with pertinent dates instead of subjects in the left-hand column.

PHYSICAL AND MENTAL EXAMINATIONS

Physical or mental examinations are appropriate in lawsuits where a person's condition is a matter of controversy, such as in personal injury litigation. FRCivP 35 requires a court order for an examination. The motion requesting the examination must specify the time, place, and scope of the exam, and name the persons who will conduct it. The results of the exam must be detailed in a written report, which is distributed to the attorneys for all parties.

REQUESTS FOR ADMISSION

FRCivP 36 sets out three categories of requests for admission: the truth of facts, the application of law to facts, and the genuineness of documents. Once a matter is admitted, it is deemed true for the purposes of the pending lawsuit and parties cannot change their minds and try to retract the admission. The purpose of requests for admission is to eliminate the need to prove at trial those matters that are not in dispute. Parties frequently admit the genuineness of documents to make the admission of evidence at trial less time-consuming. It is obviously important to answer requests for admission precisely, because the consequences of an incorrect admission can be severe.

Requests for admission may be served on the plaintiff at any time after the commencement of the lawsuit. They may be served on other parties with the summons and complaint or at any time thereafter. As a practical matter, requests for admission usually come fairly late in the discovery process, when the facts and issues have been narrowed and clarified.

Parties must serve responses within 30 days of receipt of the requests for admission, except that a defendant is allowed 45 days when the requests are served with the summons and complaint. It is imperative that paralegals enter the response deadlines in the docket control system. If a party does respond in a timely manner, the requests for admission are deemed admitted.

The format includes a caption, introductory paragraph, numbered paragraphs for each request, attorney signature, and certificate of service. It is important to state the requests precisely and word them so that the party is likely to admit their truth. Responses to requests for admission must be drafted with care. Be careful not to overlook any request or part of a request. Remember that failure to respond is deemed a conclusive admission of truth. The responses are to admit, deny, or object to the requests. A fourth response is to state why the party is unable to respond, and lack of knowledge is a suitable response only after the party has made reasonable inquiry but is still unable to respond. Paralegals help with responses by locating documents that refer to the information in the requests and by reviewing those documents.

MOTIONS FOR CONTROLLING THE DISCOVERY PROCESS

Usually the discovery process can be regulated by the attorneys without court intervention. In some cases the attorneys and the judge call a discovery conference early in the litigation to set the ground rules and basic schedule.

Occasionally, opposing attorneys reach an impasse over certain subjects. For instance, one party may refuse to answer interrogatories or may give only vague, evasive answers. An incomplete or evasive answer constitutes failure to respond. FRCivP 37 provides the procedure for enforcing discovery. The first step is for the party who requested the discovery to file a motion, asking the court to order the uncooperative party to answer the interrogatories. If the order yields no proper response, a second motion can be filed asking the court to impose sanctions on the uncooperative party. FRCivP 37(b) provides for a wide range of sanctions, which can be quite strong. The court even has the power to strike the uncooperative party's defenses and enter default judgment against them. The court can also award attorney's fees for the amount generated by the party's failure to cooperate. Review the sanctions in FRCivP 37(b), and take note of their severity. The sanctions are ample incentive to cooperate in the discovery process.

Chapter 9   Discovery

STUDY QUESTIONS

1. Define *discovery*.

2. List the five principal methods of discovery.

3. Explain the purposes of discovery.

4. What rules govern the discovery process?

5. Explain the sequence in which discovery usually takes place.

6. When must a party supplement discovery responses?

7. Explain the general scope of discovery.

8. Explain what information can be obtained about expert witnesses expected to testify at trial and expert witnesses not expected to testify at trial.

9. When is information protected from discovery?

10. Discuss how an attorney/paralegal team can plan for discovery.

11. Who answers interrogatories for a corporation or government agency?

12. At what point in the litigation may interrogatories be served?

13. How much time is generally allowed for serving answers to interrogatories?

14. What are some sources of help for paralegals drafting interrogatories?

15. List some of the usual topics for interrogatories.

16. Explain three guidelines for drafting interrogatories.

17. Discuss four guidelines for responding to interrogatories.

18. Explain acceptable bases for objecting to interrogatories.

19. Explain the procedure after interrogatories are answered.

20. Under FRCivP 34, what may a party do to another party's land?

21. If a person other than the party has the documents requested in a request for production, is this a sufficient ground for not handing over the documents?

22. How detailed a description of documents to be produced is required?

23. Explain the duties paralegals may perform in producing documents for another party's inspection.

24. Who may be required to attend a deposition?

25. What information does a notice of deposition contain?

26. What tasks may paralegals perform to prepare for depositions?

27. What tasks may paralegals perform during depositions?

28. Explain what a deposition digest is and the ways it can be arranged.

29. Explain the procedure for obtaining a physical or mental examination.

30. Explain the responses that may be given to requests for admission.

31. What is the purpose of requests for admission?

32. Explain the procedure for obtaining court sanctions against a party who refuses to cooperate with discovery.

TEST YOUR KNOWLEDGE

MULTIPLE CHOICE

1. In regard to expert witnesses, which of the following may be obtained through discovery?

    a. Bases for opinions of experts expected to testify at trial
    b. Identity of experts expected to testify at trial
    c. Bases for opinions of experts not expected to testify at trial
    d. All of the above
    e. a and b only

2. The "documents" in a request for production of documents may include which of the following?

    a. A company's business records
    b. Photographs
    c. Drawings
    d. All of the above

3. Which of the following may impose deadlines for completion of the entire discovery process?

    a. State rules of civil procedure
    b. Court order
    c. Local court rules
    d. b and c only
    e. All of the above

4. Which of the following methods may be used to protect information from discovery?

    a. Submission of information in sealed envelope kept by the court
    b. Limiting the persons who can be present at a deposition
    c. Limiting discovery to certain matters
    d. a and c only
    e. All of the above

5. A court may impose which of the following sanctions on a party who fails to cooperate with discovery?

    a. Strike the party's defenses and enter default judgment
    b. Award attorney's fees incurred as a result of the party's failure to cooperate
    c. Hold the party in contempt of court
    d. b and c only
    e. All of the above

6. Which of the following types of information are not discoverable?

    a. Information covered by the attorney-client privilege
    b. Information protected by a protective order
    c. All trial preparation materials
    d. a and b only
    e. All of the above

7. Which of the following can be subject to requests for production and inspection?

  a. A party's accounting records
  b. An electric blanket
  c. Photographs of a wrecked car
  d. a and c only
  e. All of the above

8. Which of the following are appropriate responses to requests for admission?

  a. Ignore the requests; this is deemed a denial
  b. State why the party cannot answer the request
  c. Deny the truth of the statement
  d. b and c only
  e. All of the above

9. Which of the following are appropriate formats for digests of depositions?

  a. Witness digest
  b. Chronological digest
  c. Subject matter digest
  d. b and c only
  e. All of the above

10. Requests for admission can include requests to admit which of the following?

  a. The genuineness of documents
  b. The truth of facts
  c. The application of law to facts
  d. a and c only
  e. All of the above

TRUE/FALSE

1. T F   Mental examinations are not allowed until after the examinee has completed a deposition.

2. T F   An attorney seeking an extension to answer interrogatories must file a motion with the court for an extension.

3. T F   The Federal Rules of Civil Procedure set out a sequence in which discovery methods must be used.

4. T F   Parties have to supplement answers to interrogatories when new information arises only if the new information is material.

5. T F   Because the discovery process is usually self-regulated by the attorneys, courts have no power to impose sanctions on uncooperative parties.

6. T F   Information must be admissible at trial in order to be discoverable.

7. T F   A valid ground for objection is that information sought is unduly burdensome.

8. T F   When a party fails to respond to a request for admissions, the request is deemed admitted.

9. T F   After a physical examination of a party pursuant to FRCivP 35, the doctor's report is made available only to the party's attorney.

10. T F   Persons who are not parties to the litigation can be required to answer interrogatories.

11. T F   There are no deadlines for serving answers to interrogatories.

12. T F   Depositions may be used as evidence at trial if the deponent is dead.

13. T F   Potential witnesses can be required to bring documents to depositions.

14. T F   Courts have no power to limit the number of interrogatories a party serves on another party.

15. T F   One purpose of discovery is to avoid surprises at trial.

FRCivP 26 Discovery.
  27-32 Deposition
  33 Interrogatories
  34 request for production
  35 exams (mental / physical)
  36 request for admissions
  37 Discovery disputes

Chapter 9   Discovery

ANSWERS TO STUDY QUESTIONS

1. Discovery refers to the pretrial methods by which parties to the litigation obtain information from each other so that they can prepare for trial.

2. Interrogatories, depositions, requests for production of documents and things and for entry upon land for inspection, requests for admission, and physical and mental examinations.

3. One purpose of discovery is to gather sufficient facts to prepare for trial. Another purpose is to clarify the factual and legal issues. Discovery is also used to preserve testimony for trial when the attorney/paralegal team fears that a witness will be unavailable for trial. Discovery can be used to get statements from witnesses and determine inconsistencies in the statements. Sufficient use of discovery helps to prevent surprises at trial.

4. The same rules that govern the entire litigation process control discovery—the Federal Rules of Civil Procedure, state rules of civil procedure, and local court rules. State rules generally follow the federal rules, but there can be important differences. Local court rules may impose additional requirements and deadlines. For instance, the federal rules do not require parties to file discovery materials with the court, but some state rules of civil procedure and local court rules do require filing.

5. The Federal Rules of Civil Procedure do not dictate a sequence for discovery. Discovery generally begins with interrogatories so that the parties can gather general information. Depositions usually follow so that testimony can be further developed. As it becomes evident which documents are important, requests for production are used. Requests for admission usually come near the end, after the facts and issues have been developed. Physical or mental examinations are used when it becomes evident that a party's physical or mental condition is in issue.

6. Parties are required to supplement discovery answers when a prior response is no longer accurate, such as when new information surfaces.

7. Parties may obtain through discovery any matter that is not privileged, is relevant, and is reasonably calculated to lead to evidence admissible at trial. The matter need not be admissible itself; it is sufficient if it leads to admissible evidence.

8. A party may use interrogatories to discover the identity of expert witnesses expected to testify at trial, the subject matter on which they are expected to testify, the substance of the facts and opinions about which they will testify, and a summary of the grounds on which their opinions are based. Information about experts who are not expected to testify is generally not discoverable, unless the requesting party can show exceptional circumstances that make it impracticable to obtain facts or opinions on the same subject by other means.

9. Information is protected from discovery when it is protected by privileges such as the attorney-client privilege or the work product privilege. Information can also be protected by protective orders issued by the court when disclosure would cause annoyance, embarrassment, oppression, or undue burden or expense.

10. First review the facts that your client has to establish to prevail. Then review the likely sources for the information and the best discovery method for obtaining the information. Finally, consider the expense. Discovery can be very expensive, and the client may not be able to afford all the discovery you suggest.

11. An officer or agent chosen by the corporation or government agency answers the interrogatories. That person may need to consult with others to gather all the information.

12. Interrogatories may be served on a plaintiff at any time. They may be served on other parties with the summons and complaint or afterward.

13. The usual deadline for serving responses is 30 days after the interrogatories are received, unless the interrogatories are served together with the summons and complaint, in which case 45 days are allowed.

14. Paralegals may consult office files for similar cases. Form books are available. Another source is the record on appeal in a similar case. However, paralegals must be careful to tailor the interrogatories for their own case.

15. Some frequently used topics are identity of the person answering the interrogatories, identity of witnesses, information about expert witnesses, information about pertinent documents, details of the other parties' version of events, specific information about damages, and insurance coverage. When the defendant is a corporation, a common question is whether the corporation was properly named in the pleadings.

16. Make the questions clear; ambiguous questions spawn ambiguous answers. Try to avoid questions that call for yes/no answers; you want to obtain as much information as possible. Ask the person answering the interrogatories to identify sources of information when that person does not have personal knowledge of the information given.

17. Do not volunteer any more information than is necessary. Make answers unambiguous. Do not give contradictory answers. Always consult with the attorney when questions arise.

18. Valid grounds for objection exist when the information is privileged or protected by a protective order, the question is irrelevant, the information sought is unreasonably cumulative or duplicative, or the request is unduly burdensome or expensive.

19. The attorney reviews the draft before it is finalized. The attorney and/or client sign the interrogatories, depending on requirements of local rules. The client may have to sign a verification. A copy of the answers, together with certificate of service, is served on the attorneys for all the parties.

20. The party may request permission to enter the land for inspection, and may also measure, survey, photograph, test or sample the property.

21. No. If the documents are in another person's hands, but the party has control over them, the documents are subject to production. (Otherwise, parties could avoid production simply by giving the documents to someone else to keep until the litigation is over.)

22. There is no rule that gives a specific description. The specificity of the request depends upon the nature of the litigation. Just be sure that the request is clear.

23. Paralegals first help to locate the documents. This may involve searching files at the client's office or warehouse. Paralegals then help to arrange the documents in a logical order. Before copying documents, paralegals review the documents to prevent the disclosure of protected or unnecessary information. The next step is to assign production numbers to all the documents to aid in preparing an index and in reviewing the set of documents to be sure it is complete. The numbers are stamped on the documents. Paralegals may oversee the copying of the documents and help ensure that the documents are put back in order.

24. Both parties and nonparties are subject to depositions. A nonparty can be compelled to attend a deposition by use of subpoenas. Attorneys usually depose the other parties' witnesses rather than their own. However, attorneys may depose their own witnesses if they fear the witnesses will be unavailable for trial.

25. The notice states the person to be deposed, and the date, time and place for the deposition.

26. Paralegals may arrange the room for the deposition, arrange for the court reporter, check for copying and fax availability, and draft notices of the deposition. Paralegals may also help the attorney prepare a list of questions to ask the deponent and may arrange the exhibits to be introduced.

27. Paralegals may keep the exhibits in order, take notes of the deponent's testimony, and observe the deponent's demeanor.

28. A digest is a summary of the deponent's testimony. One format is the witness digest, which is just a summary of the testimony in the order it was given. This is most appropriate for short depositions. Another format is the subject matter digest, where the subject is listed in the left-hand column and the references to the subject are listed in the right-hand column, with pages in the transcript cited. A third format is the chronological digest, set up like the subject matter digest, but with dates in the left-hand column.

29. The party seeking the examination files a motion specifying the conditions (scope) of the exam, together with details of the proposed time, place, and so on. The parties may agree on the details and enter a stipulation, obviating the need for a motion and court order. After the exam, the doctor provides details of the results to the attorneys for all parties, including diagnoses and conclusions.

30. A party may admit or deny the request. A party may also admit in part and deny in part a request, and must state this with particularity. A third response is to object to a request—for example, when the information is privileged. A fourth option is to explain why the party cannot admit or deny the request. This is appropriate only after the party has made reasonable inquiry and still cannot find out the information.

31. The purpose is to specify matters that are not in controversy, eliminating the necessity for proving these matters at trial.

32. The first step is to file a motion asking the court to order the party to respond. If the party still fails to respond, the requesting party files a second motion, asking the court to impose sanctions.

ANSWERS TO TEST YOUR KNOWLEDGE

MULTIPLE CHOICE

1. e	6. d
2. d	7. e
3. e	8. d
4. e	9. e
5. e	10. e

TRUE/FALSE

1. F	6. F	11. F
2. F	7. T	12. T
3. F	8. T	13. T
4. F	9. F	14. F
5. F	10. F	15. T

10 DOCUMENT CONTROL AND TRIAL PREPARATION

SUMMARY

In order to ensure that everything is ready for trial, a paralegal needs to know when the trial will be held. Sometimes the trial is scheduled for a particular date and time, but sometimes you know only the session or term of court in which the case will be heard. For instance, a judge may have 30 cases on the court calendar for a two-week session of civil (noncriminal) court. The judge will hear as many cases as possible during this period. Even if your case number is near the end of the list, you must be ready when the session opens; cases tend to settle quickly when they appear on a trial calendar.

A trial calendar is the court's schedule for cases to be tried. It is sometimes called the docket or trial list. The court may publish the calendar in publications to which attorneys in the area subscribe, or may mail copies of the calendar to attorneys. Sometimes attorneys pick up the calendar in the office of the clerk of court. Sometimes, particularly in federal court where one judge is assigned to the case throughout the litigation process, the judge sets a trial date during a pretrial conference.

When a case is not scheduled for a date certain, the attorney may request that the case be given a specific date for trial. This is called a peremptory setting. A peremptory setting is appropriate when important witnesses have to travel long distances to attend the trial or when other extraordinary circumstances exist.

The attorney/paralegal team should make every effort to be ready to try the case when it is scheduled. If this is impossible, the attorney may request a continuance—that is, a postponement. Of course, opposing counsel may contest the continuance. Whether the continuance is granted depends on many factors, such as the judge involved, how many times the case has been continued before, and the reason for the request.

Often trial attorneys have more than one case scheduled for trial at a given time. It is possible for attorneys to try more than one case in a day, if at least one involves a simple matter, such as an uncontested divorce. Otherwise, one of the cases will have to be continued. Local and state court rules usually provide a scheme for deciding which types of cases take precedence. For example, a trial in federal court usually takes precedence over a trial in state court.

Paralegals are often given the task of organizing the file for trial. Depending on the complexity of the case and the preferences of the attorneys who will try it, there are variations in how the file may be arranged. Organizing the file generally involves preparing an outline of the case, organizing the documents into subfiles, and developing an effective method to retrieve the documents.

In outlining the case, remember that the plaintiff's objective is to prove the essential elements of every claim asserted. The defendant's objective is to show that the plaintiff has not established all the essential elements. A good guide for outlining is your chart of essential elements. The chart should have beneath each element a list of the evidence that will be used to prove that element. A review of the chart will reveal any weaknesses in the evidence and alert the attorney/paralegal team to try to gather more. As you review the file, you can add to the list other evidence that has accumulated. For each exhibit to be used at trial, note which witness will be called on to authenticate it. Add references in discovery materials that address each of the essential elements.

An important part of preparing the file for trial is summarizing lengthy documents so that the important parts are obvious. You may already have prepared digests of depositions. Summarize other lengthy documents such as expert witness reports and discovery materials other than depositions. As you summarize documents, the headings and subheadings for your outline become clear.

It is generally necessary to divide large files into subfiles to make the documents accessible at trial. You may already have some subfiles, but you may need to rearrange some of them. You may have subfiles for particular subjects, time periods, or witnesses. Try to fit every document into an appropriate subfile. A computer search of key terms can aid you.

The next step is to prepare indices and document retrieval systems so that you can find the documents readily. Be sure that every document has been assigned a number. This is usually done as the documents are received throughout the litigation. A number gives ready identification. However, numbers do not tell you a document's content. This is why indices are necessary.

Begin developing an index by identifying index headings. Look at your outline to determine the important headings. There are two primary methods for preparing written indices. One is the manual index card system. Here you prepare an index card for each document, citing the document locator number, short description of the content, date of the document, and author. At the top of each card write the key word or category number assigned to the document. If the document is important for more than one category, assign more than one number to it. Arrange the cards by categories, and you can index the documents according to topics on the cards.

A computer document retrieval system also requires assignment of subject codes, which are entered in the computer. Other basic information about the documents is also entered, such as date, document number, and author. After the pertinent information is entered in the computer, a computer search can identify all the documents under a particular topic, and you can prepare the index.

Some attorneys like to use trial notebooks to organize for trial. A trial notebook is a binder with tabbed dividers, and in each tabbed section are the documents needed for that portion of the trial—from jury selection to closing argument. Some attorneys prefer to put all the documents to be used at trial in the notebook, if there is space. An alternative is to keep the documents in subfiles for ready access and use the trial notebook as an outline of the trial. The notebook will have, among other things, outlines of questions to ask witnesses, pertinent legal research, and outlines of opening and closing arguments.

An important pretrial task is to review the file to ensure that all documents required at trial are ready. One important document is the trial brief, sometimes called a trial memorandum or memorandum of law. The format and length of the trial brief may differ depending on local rules and dictates of the presiding judge. However, a commonly used format includes the following sections: cover or title sheet, statement of facts, questions presented, argument, and conclusion. The attorneys usually write the legal argument, but paralegals may help prepare drafts of other parts of the brief, such as the statement of facts. Paralegal tasks may also include shepardizing cases and checking case citations.

In certain types of cases the court may require the submission of standard court forms to relate financial or other information. In a child-support case, for instance, the parties may be required to submit affidavits of income and expenses. Check state and local rules to see what forms are required.

Paralegals help to prepare witnesses for trial. First inform the witnesses of the trial date and let them know that they will be subpoenaed. Paralegals can prepare the subpoenas for attorney review, make sure that the subpoenas are properly served, and then file the subpoenas with the court. All witnesses should be subpoenaed so that the court can compel their attendance, if necessary.

Paralegals may help attorneys prepare lists of questions to ask witnesses at trial. The attorneys review the questions with the witnesses before trial, and paralegals may arrange the meetings. Paralegals may sit in on the meetings to observe the witnesses and offer suggestions on how the witnesses can give more effective testimony.

There are some general guidelines for all witnesses to follow. Witnesses should always tell the truth, never answer questions until they understand the question, give no more information than is necessary, quit talking as soon as the attorney objects to a question and not resume talking until the judge rules on the objection, and review their depositions before trial.

Paralegals help prepare the exhibits for trial by arranging the exhibits in the order they will be presented and numbering them and by ensuring that sufficient copies are available for trial. Paralegals should also prepare a list of all the exhibits.

Paralegals also help prepare demonstrative evidence. Paralegals may prepare some charts themselves, and arrange for graphic artists to prepare others. Paralegals may also need to arrange for enlargements of some charts.

Paralegals also aid in jury investigation. The purpose of jury investigation is to find out background information about the potential jurors so that the attorneys can select jurors most sympathetic to their clients' version of the facts. The scope of jury investigation depends upon when the list of potential jurors is available. If the list is not available until the day before trial, little investigation can be done.

The client's litigation budget may determine the extent of investigation. Consultants are available to gather information, prepare jury profiles, and even stage mock jury trials to see how the jurors react to the evidence presented. This is expensive. If the client cannot afford this, paralegals may perform simple investigation such as checking public records to get a general idea of the jurors' background. Jury investigation should be subtle, because jurors may be offended.

Chapter 10 Document Control and Trial Preparation

STUDY QUESTIONS

1. How do lawyers inform judges that cases are ready for trial?

2. Explain the meaning of *session of court*.

3. What is a peremptory setting?

4. Who is responsible for scheduling cases?

5. What factors are important in considering whether a continuance is allowed?

6. Explain how paralegals can use the chart of essential elements to prepare for trial.

7. What should paralegals do before preparing an outline?

8. What types of documents should paralegals summarize, and why are the summaries important?

9. What categories of subfiles might be helpful?

10. Why is individual document identification important?

11. What are the two principal approaches to preparing indices of documents?

12. What is a trial notebook?

13. Describe the tasks paralegals may perform in preparing a trial brief.

14. What other documents should paralegals check during trial preparation?

15. How may paralegals help to prepare witnesses for trial?

16. How do you determine how many copies of exhibits to prepare for trial?

17. How may paralegals assist in preparing demonstrative evidence for trial?

18. How does a client's budget affect jury investigation?

TEST YOUR KNOWLEDGE

MULTIPLE CHOICE

1. Which of the following might paralegals need to summarize?

    a. Answers to requests for admission
    b. Written reports of expert witnesses
    c. Depositions
    d. All of the above
    e. b and c only

2. Which of the following helps to justify a continuance?

    a. The attorney is ill.
    b. The case has been continued twice already.
    c. The case is pending in state court and the lawyer has another case at the same time in federal court.
    d. All of the above
    e. a and c only

3. Which of the following are methods to help organize a case for trial?

    a. Prepare an outline of the case.
    b. Organize the documents in subfiles.
    c. Develop a document retrieval system.
    d. All of the above
    e. a and b only

4. Which of the following may paralegals do to prepare demonstrative evidence for trial?

    a. Arrange for a graphics company to enlarge charts.
    b. Prepare charts to illustrate points to be made at trial.
    c. Review the file for items that should be illustrated in charts.
    d. All of the above
    e. a and b only

5. Which of the following helps to determine how many copies of exhibits must be available at trial?

    a. Local court rules
    b. Judges' preferences
    c. The number of attorneys who will be present
    d. All of the above
    e. a and b only

6. Which of the following are methods by which trial dates are assigned?

    a. The trial judge announces the date in pretrial conference.
    b. The date is published in a legal newspaper.
    c. The calendar is mailed to the attorneys with cases scheduled.
    d. All of the above
    e. b and c only

7. In preparing an outline of the case, which of the following should paralegals review?

    a. The complaint
    b. Expert witnesses' reports
    c. Interrogatories
    d. All of the above
    e. a and c only

8. Which of the following are good guidelines for witnesses to follow?

    a. Always give "yes" or "no" for an answer, with no further explanation, on direct examination.
    b. When an attorney objects to a question, stop talking.
    c. Always tell the truth.
    d. All of the above
    e. b and c only

9. Which of the following statements are true?
   a. Subpoenas should be served only on the most important witnesses.
   b. Subpoenas are filed with the clerk of court after they are served.
   c. Some state courts allow the attorney, rather than the clerk of court, to issue subpoenas.
   d. All of the above
   e. b and c only

10. Which of the following aids in document retrieval?
    a. Computer search for key terms
    b. Indices of subfiles
    c. Review of discovery materials
    d. All of the above
    e. a and b only

TRUE/FALSE

1. T F   Another name for a court calendar is a docket.

2. T F   If an attorney has a case scheduled in federal court and a case scheduled in state court at the same time, the federal court case generally takes precedence.

3. T F   Index card retrieval systems work best in cases with few documents.

4. T F   Attorneys are not allowed to try more than one case on the same day.

5. T F   A certificate of readiness is a statement signed by an attorney indicating that a case is ready for trial.

6. T F   Only the clerk of court or the judge can assign a trial date.

7. T F   A period of time during which a judge is in a certain city to hear civil cases is sometimes called a term of court.

8. T F   A peremptory setting may be granted when witnesses have to travel a long distance to attend trial.

9. T F   The defendant's goal is to show that the plaintiff has established every essential element of every claim asserted.

10. T F   Paralegals may read publications by expert witnesses to spot inconsistences.

11. T F   Paralegals should not use indices for subfiles that were prepared earlier in the litigation when they formulate the document retrieval system for trial.

12. T F   A trial brief is sometimes called a trial memorandum.

13. T F   One goal of case review is to detect any weaknesses in proof.

14. T F   Trial briefs follow a rigid format that may not be altered even by local court rules.

15. T F   A paralegal task related to trial briefs may be to check case citations.

Chapter 10 Document Control and Trial Preparation

ANSWERS TO STUDY QUESTIONS

1. The lawyers may have a pretrial conference and discuss when the case will be ready for trial. Some courts have a form called a certificate of readiness that lawyers fill out and file.

2. Not all cases are scheduled for a particular day. Instead a judge has a list of cases that may be heard while the judge holds a session of court—for instance, a two-week period when the judge hears civil cases. There may be 50 cases on the judge's list, called the court calendar. Once a case is on a court calendar, it may settle quickly, so the cases at the bottom of the list could possibly be reached. Another word for *session* is *term* of court.

3. When a case is not scheduled for a particular day but rather for some day during a session of court, there may be circumstances that require a date certain for the trial. For instance, important witnesses may have to travel long distances to testify. An attorney can request a peremptory setting—that is, a specific date for trial.

4. Sometimes, particularly in federal court, the case is assigned to one judge for the entire litigation, and the judge is allowed to set the trial date. In some courts the clerk of court prepares the case schedules, and some courts have a trial court administrator to schedule cases.

5. Local rules and preferences of individual judges can influence whether a case is continued. Some judges simply do not like to continue cases. If a case has already been continued several times, another continuance is unlikely to be granted. Courts like to clear their dockets of cases that have been pending for a long time. The reason for requesting a continuance is important. If counsel is ill or has another case scheduled at the same time and that case takes precedence, a continuance will likely be granted. In contrast, if the attorney requests a continuance for a recently planned vacation, a continuance is not likely to be granted.

6. The chart of essential elements is an outline of the elements the plaintiff must establish for every claim asserted. Because the plaintiff's objective is to prove all the essential elements, paralegals should review the file to be sure that there is sufficient evidence to prove each element.

   Paralegals review the list of essential elements with the evidence listed beneath each element to show how that element is to be proven. A review of the chart reveals weaknesses in the evidence. Paralegals can review the entire file to find even more evidence to support the essential elements of each claim.

   Paralegals can list beneath each element the witnesses and exhibits that will be used to prove each element. For each exhibit, paralegals can list the witness who will be used to authenticate the document. References to other materials in the file, such as pleadings and discovery materials, can also be entered on the chart to help organize for trial.

7. It is important for paralegals to check with the attorneys who will try the case, to determine whether they have any special format or requests.

8. Paralegals should summarize any lengthy document that is significant to the case. This may include pleadings and discovery materials such as depositions and interrogatories. This may also include written statements of witnesses, including expert witnesses.

   The purpose of the summaries is to make the information readily accessible and to help organize the file for trial.

9. The categories differ depending upon the subject matter of the lawsuit and size of the file. Subfiles may be arranged according to subject matter, issues, or witnesses. The overall goal is to make all documents accessible. The exact categories should be discussed with the attorneys who will try the case. As you outline the case, the subfile categories generally become apparent. A computer search of important terms and names may also help you identify categories.

10. This can be an important part of the document retrieval system. Assigning a number to each document gives you a means of identifying each document. However, further indices are necessary to identify the content of the document for trial use.

11. One method is the manual index card system. It works best with cases that have a relatively small number of documents. To prepare the cards, review the file and identify important subject categories in which the cards will be placed. Then prepare an index card for each document. On each index card goes the document locator number, short description of the content, date, and author of the document. At the top of each card write the key word or category number assigned to the document. Multiple category numbers may be appropriate because the document is important to more than one topic. In addition to indexing by topics, cards may also be indexed by witness, date, or author.

    Computer retrieval systems are the other common method. Here you review the documents to determine the important topics for indexing. The topics are assigned subject codes, which are entered into the computer. Other information about the documents is also entered, including date, document number, and author. Once the system is set up, this information is entered for each document, and the computer can retrieve documents by topic.

12. A trial notebook is a three-ring binder with tabbed dividers. In each tabbed section are the documents needed for that portion of the trial. The notebook has sections for every stage of the trial from jury selection to closing argument. If space allows, attorneys put in the trial notebook all the documents to be used at trial. If this proves too bulky, the attorney may use subfiles for the documents and use the notebook as an outline for trial.

13. Attorneys usually write the bulk of the brief, especially the legal argument, but paralegals may help to prepare drafts of sections such as the statement of facts. Paralegals may check local rules for specific requirements for format and length. In addition, paralegals may check case citations and shepardize cases. The extent of paralegals' participation depends on the attorneys with whom they work and how much of the brief the attorneys want to do themselves.

14. In many types of cases the court requires the parties to file particular forms, usually forms that summarize evidence. For instance, in a child-support case, the court may require the parties to file affidavits of income and expenses. Sometimes the attorneys are required to prepare a pretrial order. Paralegals should ensure that all forms are completed and filed in a timely manner.

15. The first task is to inform witnesses of the trial date as soon as it is known. Paralegals should confirm the witnesses' phone numbers and addresses and inform the witnesses that they will be served with subpoenas. Paralegals may prepare the subpoenas for attorney review, and ensure that the subpoenas are properly served and then filed with the clerk of court. Paralegals may help attorneys prepare a list of questions to ask at trial. When the witnesses meet with the attorneys to review the questions, paralegals may arrange the meetings. Paralegals may observe the witnesses and offer suggestions on how they can be more effective witnesses. Paralegals may take witnesses to see the courtroom so that they will be more comfortable at trial.

16. You always need one copy for the judge and for each attorney. Keep a copy for your file as well. Local court rules or the presiding judge's instructions may require additional copies, such as a copy for the judge's law clerk.

17. Demonstrative evidence consists of charts and other visual aids to explain the facts and assist in the presentation of evidence. Paralegals may draw some of the chart themselves. They may need to arrange for graphic artists to prepare demonstrative evidence or arrange for charts to be enlarged for use at trial.

18. Jury investigation can be fairly extensive when a consultant is hired to gather background information and formulate jury profiles. The consultant may also arrange a mock jury trial. This is expensive, so not every client can afford it. Less expensive investigation may be performed by paralegals—for example, looking at public records such as tax listings to gather information on the jurors.

ANSWERS TO TEST YOUR KNOWLEDGE

MULTIPLE CHOICE

1. d	6. d
2. e	7. d
3. d	8. e
4. d	9. e
5. d	10. d

TRUE/FALSE

1. T	6. F	11. F
2. T	7. T	12. T
3. T	8. T	13. T
4. F	9. F	14. F
5. T	10. T	15. T

11 PRETRIAL CONFERENCES, ARBITRATION, AND SETTLEMENT

SUMMARY

Chapter 11 covers three areas in which paralegals are involved before trial: pretrial conferences, arbitration, and settlement.

PRETRIAL CONFERENCES

In federal court, FRCivP 16 addresses pretrial conferences. The procedure for pretrial conferences differs depending on whether a case is to be heard in federal or state court and according to local court rules and the preferences of particular judges.

In federal court, an initial pretrial conference is commonly held early in the litigation process. FRCivP 16 describes the general purposes of initial pretrial conferences: to expedite the disposition of the action, to establish early control so that the case will not be protracted, to discourage wasteful pretrial activities, to improve the quality of trial preparation, and to facilitate settlement. In the initial pretrial conference the judge sets guidelines to control the remainder of the litigation. This includes setting deadlines for completion of discovery, filing certain motions, and similar matters.

There may be multiple pretrial conferences, particularly if the parties cannot cooperate throughout the discovery process. FRCivP 16 gives judges flexibility in this and in virtually all aspects of pretrial conferences. Thus procedures vary from judge to judge. Some judges hold informal meetings with the attorneys in chambers, while others hold formal hearings in the courtroom, with a court reporter present.

The results of the pretrial conference are written in the pretrial order. This order sets forth deadlines established by the judge and contains stipulations between the parties. By stipulating to matters on which they agree, parties expedite litigation. Stipulated matters may include, for example, proper jurisdiction and proper joinder of all parties. Note that while our discussion centers on pretrial conferences with the presiding judge, federal magistrates often handle pretrial matters such as pretrial conferences.

The final pretrial conference in a federal case generally takes place several weeks before the date that the trial is scheduled. FRCivP 16 explains that the primary purpose of the final pretrial conference is to formulate a plan for trial, including a program for facilitating the admission of evidence. Settlement discussions often occur at final pretrial conferences, and some judges actively encourage settlement at the conference. Often attorneys are required to exchange information such as lists of exhibits and witnesses before the conference.

The attorneys may each prepare a proposed final pretrial order for presentation to the judge. After the conference, the judge enters a final pretrial order that includes such items as lists of contested issues, stipulations, witnesses, and exhibits. The judge also sets forth rules for the conduct of the trial, such as how many copies of exhibits to have available and the procedure for submitting proposed jury instructions. The judge may also rule on pretrial motions such as the admissibility of certain pieces of evidence.

Pretrial conferences in state court tend to cover the same topics as conferences in federal court, but often take place much closer to the time of trial. The attorneys and judge may even meet for the first and only pretrial conference on the day before trial. Pretrial conferences may range from informal discussions in chambers to formal hearings in the courtroom.

Paralegals' duties in connection with pretrial conferences may include helping to prepare lists of witnesses and exhibits and reviewing the file for any motions on which the judge still needs to rule. Paralegals also enter in the docket control system any deadlines set in the conferences. Another helpful task is to ensure that the attorneys are aware of all applicable local rules and required forms.

ARBITRATION

Arbitration is a method of dispute resolution that offers an alternative to full-blown trial. Instead of a trial, the parties select a neutral third party, the arbitrator, who reviews the evidence and issues a decision. Arbitration is gaining popularity because it is generally faster and cheaper than ordinary litigation. In fact, the purpose of arbitration is to avoid the expense, delay, and formalities of ordinary litigation.

Arbitration may be binding or nonbinding. In binding arbitration, the parties agree at the outset that they will accept the arbitrator's decision and will not seek a trial. In nonbinding arbitration, the parties are free to request a trial de novo if one of the parties is unhappy with the arbitrator's decision.

Arbitration may be mandatory or voluntary. Some courts have adopted an arbitration system in which certain types of lawsuits must be submitted to arbitration. This is mandatory arbitration. Voluntary arbitration takes place when parties choose arbitration over other options.

Arbitration may be court-annexed or private. In court-annexed arbitration, the parties follow the rules that the court has set up and are assigned an arbitrator from a list of approved arbitrators kept by the clerk of court. Private arbitration is often administered through centers that establish their own procedural guidelines and rules. Parties are also free to set up their own arbitration. For example, they may choose a panel of three experienced attorneys to hear their evidence and enter a decision.

The procedure for arbitration varies widely, depending on local rules in court-annexed arbitration and rules used by private arbitration centers. Such differences may include whether to use an arbitrator or a panel of arbitrators, whether the parties choose their own arbitrator, the level of formality at hearings, and deadlines for filing documents.

The types of cases most suitable for arbitration are civil actions in which the damages requested are not especially large. Some courts require arbitration when the damages are $150,000 or less. But like many factors related to arbitration, this can vary. Some courts require arbitration only when the damages are $50,000 or less. Remember that some courts do not require arbitration at all.

Lawsuits involving very complex or novel legal issues are not generally suitable for arbitration. In contrast, a case that deals with voluminous exhibits that a jury would have difficulty following may be a good candidate for arbitration.

Parties may submit some, but not all, issues to arbitration, if they choose. For instance, the parties may submit to arbitration on the issue of liability, but not damages.

Paralegals may perform many tasks in connection with arbitration. When a case is in arbitration, paralegals still have the usual pretrial duties of helping with discovery and with drafting pleadings and motions. Paralegal tasks during arbitration can vary according to the rules that apply to the arbitration. For example, if the rules allow only the submission of written evidence, paralegals help with written evidence but do not prepare witnesses to testify. General duties include organizing the file, helping to arrange exhibits for submission, and helping to prepare trial briefs where the rules permit them. Paralegal duties during a hearing vary according to the nature of the hearing. Some hearings are very similar to trials, and your tasks will be similar to those described in Chapter 12. Other hearings are quite simple, and you may simply take notes.

SETTLEMENT

A settlement is the resolution of a dispute by negotiation between the parties rather than by a judge or jury. The attorneys negotiate the settlement. If a party is unrepresented, the attorney deals directly with the party. Attorneys must have the clients' consent to accept a settlement offer, and the client makes the final decision. It is important to inform clients of all settlement offers. Paralegals often relate the offers to the clients, either orally or in writing. Paralegals must be careful not to advise the clients whether they should accept offers, because this constitutes rendering legal advice.

Settlement is an important topic, because more than 75 percent of all civil lawsuits are settled. Lawsuits may be settled at any time during the litigation process, including during trial.

The attorney/paralegal team must determine the settlement value of a case before entering serious settlement discussions. The settlement value is the amount the plaintiff is willing to accept and the amount the defendant is willing to pay. There is no precise formula to apply in every case. The first step is to calculate the plaintiff's damages. This can be done with some certainty for special damages, such as doctors' bills, home repairs, and lost wages. Lost wages are more difficult to determine for self-employed persons than for salaried persons, but a reasonable estimate can usually be made. General damages are more difficult to calculate because they involve less concrete concepts, such as disfigurement and pain and suffering.

The sample in our discussion in the text centers on personal injury litigation. Damages can be determined in other types of lawsuits, such as breach of contract when a party fails to repay a promissory note.

Pursuant to statute, punitive damages may be available when fraudulent or particularly egregious behavior has occurred. Punitive damages are generally three to five times the amount of compensatory damages and are awarded in addition to compensatory damages. If there is an applicable statute, it will be mentioned in your pleadings.

After calculating the amount of damages, the attorney/paralegal team subtracts the estimated amount of trial expenses. Trial expenses include fees for expert witnesses to appear, lodging and travel expenses for experts and other witnesses, copying costs, court reporter fees, and so on. If the attorneys are paid on an hourly basis, attorney's fees should be included.

The next step is to evaluate the likelihood of prevailing at trial. The less likely a plaintiff is to prevail at trial, the less is the value of the plaintiff's case. Factors to review include the strength of the evidence to prove the essential elements of all claims, the credibility of witnesses, and any outrageous conduct of the parties. Also consider any particularly sympathetic attributes of the plaintiff, such as a very young or very old plaintiff.

Finally, evaluate the likelihood of collecting the judgment. A judgment is no good unless you collect it. Examine the defendants' insurance coverage. If the insurance coverage is insufficient, investigate the defendants' assets to determine whether you can collect the judgment.

Another factor to consider is the amount of verdicts given in similar cases in the geographical area where your case is filed. Juries in large cities may award higher verdicts than juries in rural areas, where prices are less inflated. In metropolitan areas, verdicts are sometimes published. When they are not published, consult attorneys on your team or attorneys who have frequently litigated cases in the region.

Attorneys negotiate settlements in several ways. They may simply discuss the case by telephone. They may exchange offers through letters. Attorneys often conduct settlement negotiations during pretrial conferences. Clients should be available at least by telephone to give authorization for accepting offers. Negotiations often take place at the courthouse just before trial. The attorneys may shuttle between conference rooms, relaying offers to their clients.

One method of presenting a plaintiff's case for settlement discussions in a major lawsuit is a settlement brochure. The brochure gives general background on the cause of action, information on the plaintiff's background (education, employment, etc.), and summaries of the evidence on liability and damages. Some brochures are illustrated to give a more vivid picture of the damages.

FRCivP 68 addresses the offer of judgment, a formal way for defendants to make a settlement offer. In an offer of judgment the defendant states in writing the amount of the judgment that he is willing to have entered against him. If the plaintiff accepts the offer, the parties file the offer and notice of acceptance with the clerk of court, and judgment is entered. If the plaintiff rejects the offer and the judgment entered after trial is less than the amount that the defendant offered, then the plaintiff must pay the costs of trial incurred after the offer of judgment. Costs generally include marshal fees, court reporter fees, filing fees, and witness fees. Occasionally costs include attorney's fees, and then costs can become quite large. The risk of having to pay the costs encourages settlement.

Once the parties reach an agreement, it is important to reduce the terms to writing quickly. The parties may change their minds before signing agreements, and then all the hard work of negotiating is for naught. One form of recording the settlement is a consent judgment. This states the amount of damages and/or other terms and looks like a regular judgment, except that the parties and attorneys sign it, indicating their consent to the terms. Then the consent judgment is presented to the judge for approval. Judges are not required to accept the terms, but they usually do, unless the terms are outrageous. The judge signs the consent judgment, the clerk enters it, and the lawsuit is over.

A variation of the consent judgment is the consent decree. A consent decree is used generally when one party is the government and the parties agree that the defendant has engaged in illegal conduct. The consent judgment states that the party will refrain from the illegal conduct and also states any damages the defendant will pay.

Other documents for recording agreements are a stipulation of dismissal and a release or settlement agreement. The stipulation of dismissal is a simple document stating that the plaintiff dismisses the lawsuit against the defendant. The dismissal may be with prejudice, which means that the plaintiff may not later file another lawsuit concerning the same claims, or it may be without prejudice, which does not bar a later lawsuit. Usually when the parties settle all their controversies, they file a stipulation of dismissal with prejudice.

Releases and settlement agreements both state that the plaintiff will dismiss the lawsuit and state the amount of damages the defendant will pay the plaintiff. The documents release the defendant from future liability arising from the claims that the parties have settled. The release commonly states only the amount of damages, while the settlement agreement details the manner in which the damages will be paid. For instance, when the payments are made in installments, the settlement agreement will state the terms for repayment. Settlement agreements are often used for structured settlements—that is, where the plaintiff receives periodic payments instead of a lump sum.

In preparing drafts of settlement documents, paralegals must know any special requirements of the applicable jurisdiction. Often there are state laws that require that certain matters be included. Be sure to check local rules as well.

Chapter 11 Pretrial Conferences, Arbitration, and Settlement

STUDY QUESTIONS

1. Does FRCivP 16 allow judges any flexibility in the way they conduct pretrial conferences?

2. Can the course of the litigation be varied from the rules stated in the pretrial order?

3. What is the goal of the initial pretrial conference?

4. Explain the purpose of a scheduling order.

5. Explain the purpose of final pretrial conferences and the types of items usually included in final pretrial orders.

6. How might pretrial conferences in state court differ from pretrial conferences in federal court?

7. Discuss at least three paralegal duties in connection with pretrial conferences.

8. Explain the purpose of arbitration.

9. Explain the terms ''binding'' and ''nonbinding'' arbitration.

10. Is mandatory arbitration always binding?

11. Must arbitration be run by the court?

12. What are some variations that might occur in various arbitration hearings?

13. What types of lawsuits are best suited for arbitration?

14. Are there important deadlines to enter in docket control when a case is in arbitration?

15. May parties submit to arbitration on fewer than all issues in the case?

16. Describe paralegal tasks during arbitration.

17. Explain the obligation to inform clients of settlement offers.

18. Are many civil cases settled before trial?

19. Explain the meaning of the "settlement value" for a case.

20. Explain how the attorney/paralegal team determines the settlement value.

21. When and how do the parties discuss settlement?

22. Explain the general contents of settlement brochures.

23. Explain the consequences of both the acceptance and rejection of an offer of judgment under FRCivP 68.

24. What is a consent judgment?

25. What is the difference between a dismissal with prejudice and a dismissal without prejudice?

26. What is the difference between a release and a settlement agreement?

27. What is a structured settlement?

TEST YOUR KNOWLEDGE

MULTIPLE CHOICE

1. Which of the following are examples of special damages?

   a. Lost wages
   b. Disfigurement
   c. Hospital bills
   d. All of the above
   e. a and c only

2. Which of the following is a factor to consider in determining the likelihood of prevailing at trial?

   a. The credibility of witnesses
   b. The available evidence to support the essential elements of all claims
   c. The age of the plaintiff
   d. All of the above
   e. a and b only

3. Which of the following is generally included in final pretrial orders?

 a. List of plaintiff's witnesses
 b. Schedule for depositions
 c. Defendant's list of contested issues
 d. All of the above
 e. a and c only

4. Which of the following is commonly used to state the terms of settlement when the government is a party alleging that the defendant engaged in illegal conduct?

 a. Consent decree
 b. Summary judgment
 c. Consent judgment
 d. Writ of error

5. Which of the following are purposes of pretrial conferences?

 a. To expedite the disposition of the action
 b. To discourage wasteful pretrial activities
 c. To facilitate settlement
 d. All of the above
 e. a and b only

6. Which of the following are acceptable methods to choose an arbitrator?

 a. The clerk of court appoints the arbitrator.
 b. The parties choose an arbitrator from an approved list.
 c. The parties choose a panel of arbitrators.
 d. All of the above
 e. a and b only

7. Which of the following may paralegals do during settlement negotiations?

 a. Prepare summaries of evidence
 b. Help to evaluate the settlement value of the case
 c. Advise clients whether they should accept offers of settlement
 d. All of the above
 e. a and b only

8. Court costs in most cases include which of the following?

 a. Court reporter fees
 b. Attorney's fees
 c. Filing fees
 d. All of the above
 e. a and c only

9. Paralegals should enter in the docket control system which of the following?

   a. Deadlines set in pretrial orders
   b. Deadlines for seeking a trial de novo after arbitration
   c. Dates of pretrial conferences
   d. All of the above
   e. a and b only

10. Which of the following are generally included in a settlement agreement?

   a. The plaintiff's agreement to dismiss the lawsuit
   b. The amount of damages the defendant will pay the plaintiff
   c. The manner in which the damages will be paid
   d. All of the above
   e. a and b only

TRUE/FALSE

1. T F   Most lawsuits terminate at the end of a trial, not by settlement of the dispute before trial.

2. T F   Court costs usually include attorney's fees.

3. T F   State laws may impose precise requirements regarding the content of settlement agreements.

4. T F   A consent judgment has the same effect as a judgment at the conclusion of a full-blown trial.

5. T F   Civil rights actions are generally referred to arbitration.

6. T F   Lawsuits cannot be submitted to arbitration after the discovery process has started.

7. T F   In scheduling orders, magistrates often set deadlines for filing motions.

8. T F   Final pretrial conferences must be held in open court and recorded by a court reporter.

9. T F   In federal court, all cases must be submitted for mandatory arbitration unless a motion for exemption is granted.

10. T F   Results of voluntary arbitration are never binding.

11. T F   The amount of lost wages for self-employed persons cannot be calculated for purposes of settlement.

12. T F   Under the Federal Rules of Civil Procedure, an offer of judgment must be served at least 10 days before trial.

13. T F   When parties settle their dispute, they need not inform court officials until the case appears on a trial calendar.

14. T F   A purpose of pretrial conferences is to narrow the issues to be tried.

15. T F   The Federal Rules of Civil Procedure do not allow judges to rule on admissibility prior to trial.

Chapter 11   Pretrial Conferences, Arbitration, and Settlement

ANSWERS TO STUDY QUESTIONS

1. Yes, judges are allowed flexibility in the number of conferences they hold and when they hold them. Furthermore they can vary the style of their conferences from informal discussions to formal hearings in open court.

2. Yes, the litigation follows the rules in the pretrial order, but it may be modified if the pretrial order itself is modified.

3. The goal is to prepare a pretrial order that sets forth the schedule for the litigation and states the matters on which the parties agree. For instance, the parties may agree that there are no controversies regarding jurisdiction or joinder of parties. Pretrial conferences are also used to set up discovery schedules and to set certain deadlines. In addition, settlement possibilities are explored.

4. A scheduling order is entered early in the litigation and sets deadlines for such things as completion of discovery, filing and hearing motions, joining parties, and amending pleadings.

5. The overall purpose of the final pretrial conference is to narrow the issues for trial and to exchange information (e.g., lists of witnesses). This enables the trial to proceed more smoothly. Items frequently included in final pretrial orders are lists of all parties' witnesses and exhibits, stipulations on the admissibility of evidence, and lists of contested issues.

6. State rules of civil procedure and local court rules can provide different requirements for pretrial conferences. The final outcomes of the pretrial conferences are generally the same—to reach agreement on as many matters as possible, to discuss settlement, and to facilitate a smooth trial. However, the timing of the conference and the nature of the conference can differ. Often in state court there may be only one pretrial conference, and it may not occur until the day the trial is scheduled. The formality of the conference may also differ—ranging from conversations in the judge's chambers to formal hearings in open court.

7. Paralegals may gather, organize, and number exhibits. Paralegals may review the file for any motions on which the judge must still rule, keep track of deadlines set at the conferences, and ensure that attorneys know the precise federal, state, and local rules that apply.

8. The purpose of arbitration is to resolve the parties' dispute without having a full-blown trial. Arbitration is generally cheaper and faster and thus may be beneficial to the client.

9. Binding arbitration means that the parties agree to abide by the decision of the arbitrator and not seek a trial de novo if one party is unhappy with that decision. Nonbinding arbitration means that the parties do not have to accept the arbitrator's decision and may seek a trial de novo.

10. No. Mandatory arbitration means that the case must be submitted to arbitration, but it does not mean that the arbitration is binding.

11. No, court-annexed arbitration is not the only type of arbitration. Parties may elect to pursue private arbitration. This may involve the parties' choosing a panel of arbitrators and agreeing to certain procedures. In addition, parties may work through a private arbitration center, which may supply both arbitrators and procedures for arbitration.

12. Some hearings are more formal than others. Hearings can range from informal presentations to formal hearings similar to trial. The Federal Rules of Evidence may or may not apply. The parties may have a single arbitrator or a panel of arbitrators. Rules may vary regarding the submission of briefs.

13. Civil cases that do not involve huge claims for damages generally are good subjects for arbitration. For example, some courts require arbitration for civil cases involving damages of $150,000 or perhaps $50,000. Cases with complex legal issues—for example, civil rights cases—are usually not good subjects for arbitration. Cases that involve issues not litigated before are not good cases for arbitration. Cases with numerous exhibits or other factors that may confuse the jury are good cases for arbitration.

14. Yes. There may be deadlines for requesting exemption from mandatory arbitration. There may also be deadlines for filing motions and briefs. A very important deadline is the deadline for requesting a trial de novo when arbitration is nonbinding and one party is unhappy with the arbitrator's decision.

15. Yes. For instance, parties may submit to arbitration only the issue of liability or only the issue of damages.

16. Some tasks are the same as in ordinary litigation—for example, drafting pleadings and assisting with discovery. During arbitration hearings the paralegal's tasks may vary, depending on the nature of the hearing. In a simple, expedited hearing, the paralegal may just take notes. In contrast, in a more complex hearing with a lot of exhibits, the paralegal may help keep track of exhibits and assist with their presentation. Entry of deadlines in the docket control system is always an important task.

17. There is an ethical obligation to inform clients of all settlement offers. Clients make the final decision whether to accept offers, and thus it is important that every offer be conveyed to them. Paralegals often inform clients of the offers for settlement. However, it is important that paralegals never advise clients whether to accept offers. This constitutes rendering legal advice, and thus only attorneys may perform this task.

18. Yes, probably more than 75 percent of the lawsuits filed are settled. Settlement usually occurs before trial, often around the time of the final pretrial conference. However, settlement can take place at any time, even during trial.

19. The settlement value is the dollar amount for which a client will agree to settle the case. It means the amount the plaintiff is willing to accept and the amount the defendant is willing to pay.

20. There is no precise formula to use in every case. However, the first step is to calculate the amount of damages. This includes special damages, such as lost wages, and doctors' bills, and general damages, such as pain and suffering and disfigurement.

    Then you subtract from the amount of the damages the amount of trial expenses. Trial expenses include fees paid to expert witnesses to testify. Other trial expenses include lodging and travel costs for experts and other witnesses. In addition, if the attorney is being paid by the hour rather than a contingent fee, the amount of attorney's fees incurred during trial is included.

    Next the attorney/paralegal team must evaluate its client's likelihood of prevailing at trial. A number of factors must be considered, including the credibility of the witnesses and the strength of the evidence to support the essential elements of every claim. Another factor is whether any parties engaged in outrageous conduct, such as drunk driving. In addition, you must consider whether the plaintiff is particularly sympathetic. Very young and very old plaintiffs are often especially sympathetic.

An important factor is the likelihood of collecting the judgment. Entry of a judgment is not a guarantee that the plaintiff will receive the money. The defendant may have insufficient insurance. If the defendant also has few assets, the likelihood of collecting the judgment is not good.

Other miscellaneous factors include the amount of verdicts awarded by juries in the region where you will try the case. Juries in large cities may award larger verdicts than juries in small towns.

21. The parties may settle the case at any stage of the litigation. If all parties are represented by counsel, the attorneys discuss settlement, after conferring with their clients. As noted above the client makes the final decision on whether to accept a settlement offer. If a party is unrepresented, the attorney may talk directly to that party.

    The settlement discussions may be carried out in various ways. The attorneys may simply discuss the case on the telephone. They may send letters containing settlement offers. Sometimes settlement discussions take place at the courthouse just before the trial is scheduled to begin. The parties may be in conference rooms, with the attorneys shuttling back and forth to their clients with settlement offers. Particularly in large personal injury cases, the plaintiff's attorney/paralegal team prepares a settlement brochure to illustrate the plaintiff's damages.

22. The brochure generally begins with some background on how the cause of action arose. The brochure also contains information on the plaintiff's background—education, employment history, and so on. It also has summaries of the evidence on liability and on damages. This can include copies of doctors' bills, doctors' statements, and photographs, as well as any other evidence that shows the amount of the plaintiff's damages.

23. An offer of judgment is a written offer of the amount of damages the defendant is willing to have entered in a judgment against him or her. If the plaintiff accepts the offer of judgment, the parties file the offer with the clerk of court, and the clerk enters judgment against the defendant in that amount.

    If the plaintiff rejects the offer of judgment and after trial the judgment entered is less than the offer of judgment, the plaintiff must pay the costs incurred after the offer of judgment. This may include the normal court costs, but if the costs include attorney's fees, the amount can be quite large.

    The plaintiff may also give up the right to receive attorney's fees when a statute provides an award of attorney's fees to a victorious plaintiff, as in some civil rights statutes. In this instance, if the plaintiff rejects the offer of judgment, and the judgment entered after trial is smaller than the offer, then the plaintiff cannot recover from the defendant the attorney's fees the plaintiff incurred after the offer of judgment.

24. A consent judgment is one type of document that records the terms of the parties' agreement when they settle their dispute. The judgment states the amount of damages or other relief the plaintiff will receive, and the parties and their attorneys sign their consent. The consent judgment is then presented to the judge, who usually accepts the parties' agreement unless it is outrageous. The judge signs the judgment, and it is entered and becomes the final judgment in the lawsuit.

25. A dismissal with prejudice means that the plaintiff is barred from later filing another lawsuit concerning the same issues. A dismissal without prejudice does not bar the institution of a later lawsuit involving the same issues.

26. Both documents state the terms of the parties' settlement, including the amount of damages the defendant will pay the plaintiff. Both documents state that the plaintiff will dismiss the lawsuit. The difference is that a settlement agreement explains the details of how the defendant will pay the damages. For instance, when the amount of damages is large, the defendant may pay in installments over a number of years.

27. This is where the plaintiff receives periodic payments instead of a lump sum. Structured settlements are often used when the amount of damages is large.

ANSWERS TO TEST YOUR KNOWLEDGE

MULTIPLE CHOICE

1. e	6. d
2. d	7. e
3. e	8. e
4. a	9. d
5. d	10. d

TRUE/FALSE

1. F	6. F	11. F
2. F	7. T	12. T
3. T	8. F	13. F
4. T	9. F	14. T
5. F	10. F	15. F

12 TRIAL

SUMMARY

INTRODUCTION

Trial is the culmination of all the months of pretrial preparation performed by the attorney/paralegal team. Each party is ready to convince the finder of fact that its version of the facts is true. The finder of fact in jury trials is the jury, and in nonjury trials is the judge.

The litigation may still be settled even during the trial. Therefore there is still a chance that more negotiations will take place.

THE COURTROOM

The general layout of courtrooms is for the judge to sit behind a raised desk-like structure called the bench. The bench is at the front, and the jury box is on the side of the courtroom. Tables for the attorneys for each party are in front of the bench, though some distance back. Sometimes attorneys ask to approach the bench to talk to the judge. When both attorneys advance to discuss something with the judge, this is a bench conference.

Some courts require the attorneys to stay behind their tables at all times, except for opening and closing arguments. Other courts allow the attorneys to move about the courtroom at will.

TRIAL PROCEDURE

Trials tend to follow an established procedure; that is, the stages of the trial occur in a set pattern.

The first step is the final pretrial conference with the judge. If the trial is in federal court this has probably already been done. However, in state court the final pretrial conference is often held on the first day of trial. The purpose of this last conference is to discuss settlement possibilities, to have the judge rule on motions such as admissibility of certain evidence, and to let the judge give special instructions to the attorneys, if necessary. Some judges have casual conferences in their chambers and others have formal hearings in a courtroom. The motions decided before trial are called motions *in limine*—that is, on the threshold of trial.

Jury Selection

The group of persons from whom the jury will be chosen is called the jury pool and consists of adults residing in the jurisdiction chosen at random. The attorneys must choose a jury, and this process is called voir dire.

Some courts require juries to be comprised of twelve persons, and other courts allow juries of as few as six persons. The purpose of voir dire is to get basic information about the potential jurors—education, occupation, family status, and so on. Sometimes jurors are asked their opinions about certain pertinent issues. The attorneys for each party want to pick the jurors that they feel are most likely to find in favor of their client. Sometimes the judge asks the questions, and sometimes the attorneys do. This varies according to local court rules and judges' preferences.

Attorneys excuse a potential juror when they feel that the person would not favor their client. An attorney excuses a potential juror by exercising a challenge—that is, stating a request that the person be excused from the jury. There are two types of challenges. In a peremptory challenge the attorney simply excuses the juror and does not have to explain why. The number of peremptory challenges is limited, sometimes to three. In a challenge for cause the attorney states why the potential juror should be excused—for example, because the person exhibited some type of prejudice. There is no limitation on the number of challenges for cause.

During voir dire, paralegals keep a chart of the jury seats and strike persons' names as they are excused. The final chart shows the jury that has been selected.

Opening Statements

The plaintiff's attorney usually gives the first opening statement. An opening statement is a forecast of the evidence that the plaintiff will present. The purpose is to show the jury from the outset that your client's version of the facts is correct. The defendant's attorney's opening statement follows. Unlike closing arguments, opening statements are not argumentative.

Presentation of Plaintiff's Case

The plaintiff has the burden of proof—that is, the plaintiff must prove the essential elements of each claim asserted by the ''preponderance of the evidence.'' This means that the jury finds the plaintiff's version of the facts more probable than not.

The two primary ways to present evidence are by testimony of witnesses and introduction of documentary evidence. The plaintiff's attorney calls the witness and conducts direct examination, asking open-ended questions and allowing the witness to tell the story. Attorneys are not supposed to use leading questions on direct examination. Leading questions are questions that imply that there is only one correct answer to the question, generally either yes or no. Leading questions are used on cross-examination. This is when the defense attorney examines the plaintiff's witnesses and tries to undermine their testimony and question their credibility. After cross-examination, the plaintiff's attorney is allowed to conduct redirect examination. This is generally a series of short questions to explain answers given on cross-examination and to try to rehabilitate the witness—that is, to undo any damage done on cross.

All documents to be presented are labeled. They may be labeled before trial if the attorneys have agreed, or they may be numbered by the clerk assisting the judge during trial. The general procedure is the same for all parties. First the attorney lays a foundation—that is, establishes the document's relevance by questioning a witness about it. The attorney then hands a copy to opposing counsel, has the clerk affix the official court label, and hands a copy to the judge. The attorney must also establish the document's authenticity. Frequently the attorneys agree before trial to stipulate to the genuineness of certain documents. At the end of the presentation of documentary evidence, the attorney requests the judge to enter the documents into evidence. This means that the jury can review the documents and take them during deliberations. The opposing counsel can object to the entry of the documents, for instance, if there is a question of authenticity.

Attorneys object to the admission of testimony and documentary evidence throughout the trial. They must state their reason for objection—for example, that the evidence is hearsay and fits no hearsay exception. The presenting attorney states why the evidence is admissible, and the judge rules on whether the evidence may be admitted. It is important for witnesses to stop talking as soon as an attorney objects and not to start again until the judge has ruled. Attorneys who think the judge erred in admitting evidence must save this, along with any other grounds for appeal, until the conclusion of the entire trial.

A motion for directed verdict is granted when the plaintiff has not presented a *prima facie* case—that is, sufficient facts for the jury to find in favor of the plaintiff. If the plaintiff has not presented enough evidence to be the basis of a favorable verdict, the judge can take the case away from the jury, enter a verdict in favor of the defendant, and send the jury home. The plaintiff also moves for a directed verdict at the close of the defendant's evidence.

Presentation of Defendant's Case

The procedure for presenting the defendant's case is the same as for the plaintiff—direct examination, cross-examination, and redirect examination. The defense attorney strives to show weaknesses in the plaintiff's case without appearing too defensive. A defendant who has asserted a counterclaim must establish a prima facie case for the claim. At the end of presenting evidence, defense counsel moves to enter the defendant's exhibits into evidence.

Rebuttal Evidence, Closing Motions, and Closing Arguments

After the defendant has rested its case, the plaintiff may present rebuttal evidence. This evidence is usually short, and its aim is to rebut specific points made by the defendant.

At the close of the rebuttal evidence, the plaintiff moves for a directed verdict. The defendant renews the motion for a directed verdict.

Attorneys for both sides now deliver their closing arguments. A closing argument is a summary of the evidence presented, given in a manner that persuades the jury that your client's version of the facts is true. Closing arguments can be dramatic if an attorney has a flair for drama and a case with some emotional appeal. The plaintiff's attorney usually goes first.

Jury Instructions, Deliberation, and Verdict

The jury's responsibility is to determine which facts it believes are true and then apply the law to those facts. The judge instructs the jury by explaining the law that must be applied. Judges usually read a fairly standard set of written instructions, depending on the subject matter of the case. Attorneys may submit special instructions and request that the judge use them. If the judge gives erroneous or incomplete instructions, this can be a ground for appeal.

While the jury is deliberating, it may have more questions for the judge. The written questions are sent out of the jury room for the judge's answer.

The jury returns to the courtroom for announcement of the verdict, which may be one of two principal types. In a special verdict the jury must answer specific written questions for each issue of fact. In a general verdict the jury reports only the party who wins and the amount of the award. A hybrid of the two is a general verdict with answers to interrogatories that ask the jury to state its conclusions about certain issues of fact.

Entry of Judgment

The judge announces the judgment in open court. Then a written judgment is prepared and filed so that the clerk of court can enter the judgment. There are various procedures for preparing the written judgment; sometimes the judge's law clerk prepares it, and sometimes the prevailing party's attorney does. At the conclusion of the trial, attorneys may make post-trial motions.

Differences Between Jury and Nonjury Trials

Nonjury trials are simpler because there are fewer steps. The procedure is basically the same for introduction of evidence. One important procedural difference is that at the end of the plaintiff's evidence the defendant moves not for a directed verdict, but for an involuntary dismissal, pursuant to FRCivP 41(b).

PARALEGAL DUTIES AT TRIAL

Paralegals have many important tasks to perform throughout the trial. Paralegals are invaluable at trial because they are often at least as familiar with the case as the attorneys are. Their knowledge of the documents is sometimes greater than the attorney's.

Paralegals are often responsible for ensuring that witnesses are present and on time. You inform witnesses of the time to arrive at the courtroom and keep a log of witnesses presented.

One important task is taking notes of questions asked and answers given. You may also keep an outline of the questions that the attorney plans to ask and alert the attorney if any questions are skipped. While attorneys are busy questioning, paralegals can spot inconsistencies in a witness's testimony and point out where the contradictory testimony appeared—for example, in a deposition.

Paralegals help attorneys keep exhibits in the order in which they will be introduced at trial. Paralegals also keep lists of exhibits presented and entered into evidence. If some exhibits have not been entered into evidence, the paralegal brings this to the attorney's attention. At the end of each trial day, the paralegal ensures that the attorney/paralegal team has a complete set of all exhibits entered by both sides.

Legible notes are essential. When there is no daily transcript prepared by a court reporter, the paralegal must keep accurate notes of every significant question, answer, and event that happens at trial.

Paralegals should observe the jurors to detect adverse reactions to the attorney or to certain witnesses. Paralegals can also note the judge's reactions. Attorneys may be so busy thinking about the next question to ask that they are unable to make these observations.

Practical tips: Take extra office supplies to the courtroom. Be prepared for long days, surprises, and missed lunches!

Chapter 12   Trial

STUDY QUESTIONS

1. May a lawsuit be settled once the case is scheduled for trial?

2. Describe the typical layout of a courtroom.

3. Explain how final pretrial conference procedures vary between state and federal court.

4. What is the purpose of voir dire?

5. What is the purpose of the opening statement?

6. Explain the burden of proof that the plaintiff must meet.

7. How does direct examination differ from cross-examination?

8. Explain the steps attorneys follow to introduce documentary evidence.

9. What must a plaintiff establish to survive a motion for a directed verdict?

10. What special considerations do defendants have when presenting their evidence?

11. What motions do the attorneys make at the close of evidence in a jury trial?

12. What is the purpose of closing arguments?

13. What sources do judges use for jury instructions?

14. Why is it important that jury instructions be accurate?

15. What is the difference between a general verdict and a special verdict?

16. Describe two differences between jury and nonjury trials.

17. Explain how paralegals ensure that witnesses are present when needed.

18. How are paralegals' trial notes used at trial?

19. How do paralegals help in the orderly presentation of exhibits?

20. What observations made by paralegals during trial are helpful?

TEST YOUR KNOWLEDGE

MULTIPLE CHOICE

1. In a jury trial, at the end of the plaintiff's evidence, the defendant usually moves for

   a. a directed verdict.
   b. involuntary dismissal.
   c. summary judgment.
   d. Any of the above

2. Jurors are selected in which of the following?

   a. The final pretrial conference
   b. Stare decisis
   c. Voir dire
   d. None of the above

3. Which of the following may occur in the final pretrial conference?

   a. Judges and attorneys discuss settlement possibilities.
   b. Attorneys state changes in witnesses they will present.
   c. The judge grants motions for a directed verdict.
   d. All of the above
   e. a and b only

4. Which of the following statements about cross-examination are true?

   a. The attorney may ask leading questions.
   b. The attorney is not allowed to ask leading questions.
   c. The attorney may impeach the witness.
   d. All of the above
   e. a and c only

5. Which of the following must attorneys do in presenting exhibits at trial?

   a. Establish the authenticity of the document.
   b. Give a copy of the exhibit to the judge.
   c. Lay a foundation to show that the exhibit is relevant.
   d. All of the above
   e. b and c only

COMPLETION

1. When the attorneys approach the judge to discuss a matter in court, this is called a _____.

2. The group from which the jury is selected is called the _____.

3. Motions made in pretrial conferences are called motions _____.

4. When an attorney excuses a juror without stating a reason, this is called a _____.

5. A verdict in which the jury reports only which party prevails and the amount of damages is called

   a _____ verdict.

TRUE/FALSE

1. T F   Judges are allowed to rule on evidentiary motions before trial.

2. T F   When a judge overrules an objection to the admission of evidence, an attorney should file an immediate appeal.

3. T F   Attorneys may exercise an unlimited number of challenges for cause.

4. T F   Attorneys are allowed to submit to the judge requests for special jury instructions.

5. T F   After presentation of the plaintiff's and defendant's evidence, the parties are no longer allowed to consider settlement.

6. T F   Incomplete jury instructions can be a ground for appeal.

7. T F   Rule 611 of the Federal Rules of Evidence dictates a specific procedure that trials must follow.

8. T F   Opening statements are generally argumentative.

9. T F   After a verdict is returned, no more motions are allowed.

10. T F   In most civil cases, plaintiffs must prove their claims by the preponderance of the evidence.

Chapter 12   Trial

ANSWERS TO STUDY QUESTIONS

1. Yes, a settlement may be reached during the final pretrial conference or during the actual trial.

2. The judge sits at the front of the courtroom at a raised desk-type structure called the bench. The jury sits in the jury box at one side of the courtroom. The attorneys for each party sit at tables that face the judge except during the portions of the trial that they are allowed to stand at other places in the courtroom.

3. Federal court conference procedure usually differs from that of state court. In federal court the common practice is to schedule a formal final pretrial conference several weeks before trial. In state court the conference frequently does not take place until the first day of trial. Therefore the attorneys and judge may discuss settlement then for the first time. In addition, individual judges have preferences for both the conduct and timing of the conference.

4. Voir dire is the process for selecting the jury from the jury panel. The judge and/or attorneys ask the potential jurors questions about aspects of their background: family, education, occupation, and so on. Questions about specific issues pertinent to the trial may also be asked. The purpose is to pick a jury that is most likely to be favorable to your client.

5. In their opening statements the attorneys give the jury a preview of the evidence they will present. The attorneys interweave with the forecast of evidence an explanation of the facts the client will prove and the theory that justifies holding for their client.

6. Plaintiffs must convince the finder of fact that they have proven all essential elements of their claims by the preponderance of evidence. Preponderance of the evidence does not mean that the jury must have no doubt that the plaintiffs have established their claims. It means that it is more probable than not that the facts are as the plaintiffs contend.

7. Direct examination is examination of a witness by the attorney who called the witness to the stand. The attorney may not use leading questions. The purpose is to present a convincing version of the facts. Cross-examination is examination of a witness by opposing counsel, who is allowed to ask leading questions. The purpose of cross-examination is to undermine the witness's testimony—for example, by pointing out inconsistencies.

8. The attorney first lays a foundation by testimony of a witness that establishes the relevance of the exhibit. Then the attorney gives a copy to opposing counsel, has the judge's clerk label the exhibit, and presents one copy to the judge and one to opposing counsel. The attorney must also establish the document's authenticity if there is no stipulation as to genuineness. At the close of evidence, the attorney moves that all exhibits be entered into evidence, which means that the jury can consider the exhibits during deliberations.

9. The plaintiff must establish a prima facie case, that is, sufficient evidence to allow the jury to rule in the plaintiff's favor. If the judge determines that the plaintiff has not presented sufficient evidence, the judge may grant the motion for a directed verdict, which ends the lawsuit.

10. Defendants try to show the weaknesses in the plaintiff's evidence by emphasizing the strengths of their own evidence. Defendants who filed counterclaims have the burden of proof to establish the claim, just as plaintiffs do.

11. The plaintiff moves the court to enter a directed verdict against the defendant. The defendant renews the earlier motion for a directed verdict.

12. Closing arguments are summaries of the evidence presented at trial, and the attorney tries to show that the facts are as his or her client asserted. The attorney interweaves the theory on which his or her client should prevail.

13. Most states have developed standard jury instructions for different types of cases, and judges frequently use these. Judges may also include special requests from the attorneys.

14. It is important that the jury know the applicable law, which is the purpose of jury instructions. The jury must be able to apply the appropriate law to the facts. Also, insufficient or incorrect instructions may be a ground for appeal.

15. A general verdict states only the amount of damages to which the prevailing party is entitled. Of course, if the defendant wins, that amount is zero. In a special verdict, the jury must answer specific written questions for each issue of fact.

16. In a jury trial the jury is the finder of fact, and in a nonjury trial the judge is the finder of fact. An example of a procedural difference is that in a jury trial, the defendant moves for a directed verdict at the close of the plaintiff's evidence. In a nonjury trial, the defendant moves for an involuntary dismissal at the close of the plaintiff's evidence.

17. Paralegals inform witnesses of the date and time to arrive in court. They keep a log of witnesses who testify so that they know which witnesses are coming up.

18. The notes can be used to spot inconsistencies in the testimony and to plan cross-examination of the witness. The notes can be reviewed during evening planning sessions between trial days. The notes may also be used in determining grounds for appeal.

19. Paralegals keep lists of the exhibits presented and entered into evidence. They keep the documents in the order in which they will be introduced. They ensure that adequate copies are available.

20. Observations of reactions of jurors and judges to witnesses and attorneys are helpful. The attorneys frequently are too busy to notice facial expressions and other indicators of feelings.

ANSWERS TO TEST YOUR KNOWLEDGE

MULTIPLE CHOICE

1. a

2. c

3. e

4. e

5. d

COMPLETION

1. bench conference

2. jury panel

3. in limine

4. peremptory challenge

5. general

TRUE/FALSE

1. T	6. T
2. F	7. F
3. T	8. F
4. T	9. F
5. F	10. T

13 POST-TRIAL PROCEDURES AND APPEALS

SUMMARY

POST-VERDICT MOTIONS

The trial is over, but this does not mean you are ready to close your file. Inevitably one party will be unhappy with the trial outcome. The unhappy party can file post-verdict motions, the most common of which are motion for a judgment notwithstanding the verdict and motion for a new trial. A party may file either or both motions.

The motion for judgment notwithstanding the verdict (JNOV) is governed by FRCivP 50(b). A prerequisite for filing a motion JNOV is that the party moved for a directed verdict during the trial. The motion for JNOV must be filed within 10 days of entry of judgment. The motion asks the judge to set aside the jury's verdict on the premise that it is not supported by sufficient evidence. The judge must determine whether there is sufficient evidence to support the jury's verdict, and in making this determination considers the evidence in the light most favorable to the party against whom the motion is made.

A dissatisfied party may also file a motion for a new trial, which is governed by FRCivP 59. FRCivP 59 does not state specific grounds that justify a new trial; rather, it states that a new trial may be granted for the reasons that courts have used before to grant new trials. Thus the attorney/paralegal team must research the grounds that have been used before as the basis for a new trial. Examples of grounds for granting new trials include excessively high or low damages, misconduct by the attorneys during trial, obvious failure of the jury to follow the judge's instructions, and newly discovered evidence. A motion for a new trial must be filed no later than ten days after entry of judgment.

It is important to understand that a motion for a new trial is not the same as filing an appeal. In an appeal, the appellate court reviews what happened at trial and determines whether prejudicial errors occurred. In a motion for a new trial, the trial judge is asked to review the trial to determine whether prejudicial errors sufficient to warrant a new trial occurred.

An important concept in motions for a new trial and in appeals is harmless error. Not every error made at trial warrants a new trial. FRCivP 61 provides that the court must disregard any procedural error that does not affect the substantial rights of the parties. Whether an error is harmless is open to interpretation, so legal research is in order.

JUDGMENTS

A judgment is the court's final decision; it resolves all matters in dispute among the parties to the litigation. At the conclusion of a trial, the judge announces the judgment to be entered. The judgment must then be reduced to writing and signed by the judge. In a federal court action it is often the judge's law clerk who drafts the judgment. Sometimes the judge asks the attorneys to draft the judgment. In that case the attorney for the prevailing party usually drafts the judgment, gives it to the other attorney to review, and then presents it to the judge for signature. The practice of having the attorneys draft the judgment is common in state courts, where most judges do not have law clerks.

Judgments vary in length, depending on the complexity of the case. It is important that judgments be accurate and complete, because a mistake or omission is a ground for appeal. The format for judgments is uniform: an opening paragraph stating the name of the judge and the session of court in which the trial was conducted; Findings of Fact, which state the facts that the court finds to be true; Conclusions of Law, which state the applicable law upon which the judgment is based; and finally the statement of the relief granted to the parties—for example, how much money the defendant must pay to the plaintiff. The final section also states which party bears the costs. Often the trial transcript is not ready when the judgment is drafted, so the attorney/paralegal team must rely heavily on the paralegal's notes taken at trial.

The judgment becomes effective only when it is entered as provided in FRCivP 79. The judge signs the judgment, and the judgment is filed with the clerk of court. The clerk of court then enters the judgment in the judgment book, called the civil docket. The entry is a short statement of the parties, court file number, date the entry is made, and the substance of the judgment. The civil docket is a multivolume series of books, usually divided into judgments entered in a certain time period—for example, 1980–1990. The civil docket contains a multivolume index for each time period; judgments are indexed there under both plaintiffs' and defendants' names.

Completed at the end of trial is a form known as the bill of costs. This is generally a standard, preprinted form available from the clerk. The prevailing party tallies the court costs, which generally include filing fees, witness fees, fees for service of pleadings, and fees for court reporters. If there is not a standard fee, then the costs must be reasonable. Check with the clerk of court to see whether there are standard fees.

Enforcement of judgments is an important topic, because a judgment is not always paid just because it has been entered in the civil docket. Often the nonprevailing party pays the judgment in a timely manner, especially when there is sufficient insurance coverage. However, sometimes it is necessary to go through the formal process of collecting the judgment, known as execution. Other important terms are judgment creditor, the party to whom the judgment is paid, and judgment debtor, the party who is supposed to pay the judgment.

However, execution cannot be successful if the judgment debtor has disposed of or transferred all assets to avoid paying the judgment. The attorney/paralegal team can take steps at the beginning of the litigation to prevent disposal of assets. FRCivP 64 allows a party to use the remedies available under state law or any applicable federal statute. Common remedies include attachment, when the sheriff seizes the defendant's personal property and keeps it, pending the outcome of the litigation. Another remedy is to file a notice of lis pendens, which is a short statement that real property is the subject of litigation. The notice of lis pendens is put in the civil docket and warns potential buyers that the real property is the subject of litigation. After the judgment is paid, the notice of lis pendens is cancelled.

FRCivP 64 provides that the procedure for execution on a judgment is the procedure of the state in which the district court is held. If a federal statute applies, the federal statute is followed to the extent that it is applicable. Most often, the state procedures apply. The text walks you through an example of the procedure for execution. The procedures may differ among states.

The procedure for execution differs also according to whether the judgment debtor is an individual or a corporation. Individual judgment debtors are allowed at the beginning of the execution process to claim certain property as exempt from execution. In our example, the judgment debtor is first served with notice that the judgment has been entered and that he is allowed to file a schedule of exempt property. If the judgment debtor fails to file a schedule of exempt property within the allotted time, then execution can take place without a further hearing. If the judgment debtor files a schedule of exempt property and request for exemption, then a hearing is held to determine what property is in fact exempt under the applicable law. Magistrates often preside at these hearings.

The actual execution involves seizing and selling the judgment debtor's nonexempt property to satisfy the judgment. For example, a car owned by the judgment debtor may be seized and sold, with the proceeds applied to pay the judgment.

Sometimes the attorney/paralegal team feels that judgment debtors have not disclosed all their property. FRCivP 69 allows the judgment creditor to conduct post-trial discovery to gain information about a judgment debtor's assets. Interrogatories are the primary means for securing information. Paralegals may review public records such as tax listings to search for the judgment debtor's assets.

A final important concept is the judgment-proof defendant. If the defendant does not have sufficient insurance coverage and does not have property to execute against, then the judgment cannot be collected. This is a judgment-proof defendant. It is wise to investigate the defendant's assets before filing a lawsuit. If a review of the civil docket reveals numerous unpaid judgments entered against the potential defendant, you may go through the time and expense of litigation for naught.

APPEALS

When a party is unhappy with the judgment entered, the party may appeal— that is, have an appellate court review the proceedings to determine whether there were reversible errors. Reversible errors are errors made by the trial court that deprive a party of a fair trial.

Before filing, the attorney/paralegal team must assess whether an appeal is worthwhile. Appeals are time-consuming and expensive, so the team must assess its likelihood of winning an appeal. This depends in large part on the seriousness of the errors committed during the trial. The client makes the final decision to appeal, but the attorney/paralegal team must analyze whether an appeal is worthwhile and advise the client wisely.

Once a case is appealed, the appellate court has jurisdiction, and the rules of appellate procedure for that court apply. In federal appellate courts the Federal Rules of Appellate Procedure apply. They are supplemented by internal operating procedures of the circuit courts of appeal, which are analogous to local court rules. In state court, the state's rules of appellate procedure apply.

The party who appeals the case is the appellant. The party who asserts that the trial court's actions were correct is the appellee.

An important concept for appeals is the final decision rule. Numerous errors may be committed at trial. However, the trial cannot stop for every alleged error so that an appeal can be taken. Rather, the appellant must wait until after the trial court's final judgment is entered and then take up one appeal that addresses all the alleged reversible errors. The final decision rule requires the appellant to wait until entry of the court's final decision before filing an appeal. The court's orders entered before the final decision are called interlocutory orders. Interlocutory orders can be appealed only in certain narrow circumstances. Basically, the trial judge has to certify that an immediate appeal is necessary. Otherwise, no issues can go up on appeal until after entry of the court's final decision.

The function of appellate courts is not to retry the case. Rather, the appellate courts examine the record on appeal to determine whether any reversible errors occurred at trial. The record of appeal contains the original papers and exhibits filed in the trial court, the transcript of proceedings, if any, and a certified copy of the docket entries prepared by the clerk of the district court. The appellate court may either affirm (uphold) the trial court's decision or reverse (overturn) it, remanding the case for correction of the errors.

It is important to follow the applicable rules of appellate procedure to the letter. It is also important to maintain an accurate docket control system, because the rules of appellate procedure impose strict filing deadlines.

An overview of the Federal Rules of Appellate Procedure is helpful. First the appellant files a notice of appeal, a short statement that the appellant is filing an appeal with the appropriate appellate court. The notice of appeal must be filed within 30 days of entry of the judgment from which the appeal is taken. If the United States government is the appellant, 60 days are allowed. When an appellant seeks permission to appeal an interlocutory order, the appellant must file a request for permission to appeal within 10 days of entry of the order from which the appeal arises.

The notice of appeal is filed with the clerk of the trial court, who sends a copy to the clerk of the appellate court. The appellate court clerk enters the appeal on the docket. Some circuit courts of appeal have internal operating procedures that require filing of a docketing statement that gives general information about the nature of the case on appeal.

There are costs assessed for appeals, including the cost of duplicating briefs and docketing fees. The appellant may be required to post a bond to cover these costs. If the decision of the lower court is affirmed, the appellant generally has to pay the costs. If the decision of the lower court is reversed, the appellee generally has to pay the costs.

An important part of the record on appeal is the transcript of the trial court proceedings. FRAP 10 requires the appellant to obtain a copy of all or pertinent parts of the transcript from the court reporter, and the transcript is made part of the record on appeal. The FRAP impose deadlines for ordering the transcript from the court reporter and deadlines for the court reporter to submit the transcript to the appellate court.

Appellate briefs are of critical importance, because they are the primary tool for convincing the appellate court either to reverse or affirm the trial court's decision. The Federal Rules of Appellate Procedure and internal operating procedures impose precise requirements for format and length. These requirements must be followed to the letter. In preparing appellate briefs, paralegals perform many of the same tasks as with trial briefs—drafting a statement of facts, conducting legal research, shepardizing cases, checking citations, and proofreading.

FRAP 30 requires preparation of an appendix to the brief. The appendix must include the relevant docket entries from the proceeding from which you are appealing; relevant portions of the pleadings, charge, findings, or opinion; the judgment or order in question; and any other parts of the record to which the parties wish to direct the court's attention.

There are three briefs filed in an appeal. The appellant's brief explains why the trial court committed reversible error. The appellee's brief responds, explaining why the trial court's decision should be affirmed. Then the appellant is allowed to file a reply brief, responding to the appellee's brief. The FRAP impose deadlines for filing each of the briefs, and the deadlines must be entered in the docket control system.

Oral argument is when the attorneys appear before the appellate court and argue the strongest points in favor of their position. Oral argument is usually short, and lawyers have time only to emphasize the most important points. The appellate court may waive oral argument. Oral argument in the circuit courts of appeal is addressed to a three-judge panel. The number of judges or justices before whom attorneys argue differs in state courts.

After oral argument, the judges who heard the arguments hold conferences to determine how they will rule, and the case is assigned to one judge to write the opinion. When the opinion is out, the clerk of the appellate court enters the court's judgment and sends a copy of the judgment to the parties. The court does not always issue a written decision.

The party that fails to prevail may file a petition for rehearing. The party may also request a rehearing en banc—that is, before all the judges on the court, not just the three-judge panel that heard the first oral argument. These petitions are not frequently granted and should be filed only when there is a compelling argument.

Chapter 13 Post-Trial Procedures and Appeals

STUDY QUESTIONS

1. When may a judge grant a motion for judgment notwithstanding the verdict?

2. What guidelines do the Federal Rules of Civil Procedure give for granting motions for new trial?

3. Why is a harmless error not a viable ground for appeal?

4. How does a judgment differ from an interlocutory order?

5. Who drafts the judgment?

6. What are the general contents of a judgment?

7. When does a judgment become effective?

8. What is the bill of costs?

9. Describe two ways to prevent a judgment debtor from disposing of assets prior to execution.

10. What is a self-executing judgment?

11. What procedure does a judgment creditor follow to enforce a judgment obtained in federal district court?

12. How does execution on a judgment against an individual differ from execution on a judgment against a corporation?

13. Why is it a good idea to investigate a defendant's insurance coverage and assets at the outset of the litigation process?

14. What are factors to consider to determine whether an appeal is worthwhile?

15. Why are interlocutory orders usually not immediately appealable?

16. How does the function of appellate courts differ from trial courts?

17. In an appeal taken to the Fourth Circuit Court of Appeals, which rules of procedure apply?

18. Describe the procedure for filing a notice of appeal.

19. What does the clerk of the trial court do with the notice of appeal?

20. Do the Federal Rules of Appellate Procedure impose deadlines for filing the transcript of the trial?

21. What tasks do paralegals perform in connection with appellate briefs?

22. Do appellate rules impose any requirements for appellate briefs?

23. Describe the three types of appellate briefs generally allowed.

24. Why do attorneys not repeat their entire argument in the oral argument?

TEST YOUR KNOWLEDGE

MULTIPLE CHOICE

1. What is the party who owes payment of judgment to the prevailing party called?

    a. The judgment creditor
    b. The defendant
    c. The judgment debtor
    d. None of the above

2. Which of the following is a valid ground for appeal?

   a. A harmless error
   b. A reversible error
   c. A judgment without sufficient conclusions of law
   d. All of the above
   e. b and c only

3. What is a written notice stating that a piece of real property is the subject of litigation called?

   a. Notice of lis pendens
   b. Notice of appeal
   c. Attachment
   d. Writ of execution

4. The clerk of court enters judgments in which of the following?

   a. Appeals docket
   b. Civil docket
   c. Court calendar
   d. Writ of execution

5. Which of the following are court costs at the trial court level?

   a. Court reporter fees
   b. Filing fees
   c. Witness fees
   d. All of the above
   e. a and c only

6. Which of the following is part of the appendix to the appellate brief?

   a. The judgment in question
   b. Relevant parts of the pleadings
   c. Relevant parts of the instructions to the jury
   d. All of the above
   e. a and b only

7. Which of the following may be grounds for granting a motion for a new trial?

   a. Misconduct by attorneys at trial
   b. Newly discovered evidence
   c. Other reasons that courts have used before to grant new trials
   d. All of the above
   e. b and c only

8. A judgment becomes effective when which of the following occurs?

   a. The judge signs it
   b. The judge pronounces it in open court
   c. The clerk of court enters it in the civil docket
   d. Execution is complete

9. Pursuant to FRAP 31, the appellee has how many days to file a brief?

    a. 40 days from service of the appellant's brief
    b. 30 days from service of the appellant's brief
    c. 10 days from service of the appellant's brief
    d. 30 days from filing of notice of appeal

10. What is the process for enforcing payment of a judgment called?

    a. Attachment
    b. Entry of judgment
    c. Execution
    d. Writ of coram nobis

TRUE/FALSE

1. T F   Oral argument may be waived by the appellate court.

2. T F   The Bill of Costs is generally prepared by the prevailing party.

3. T F   A prerequisite for filing a motion for judgment notwithstanding the verdict is moving for a directed verdict.

4. T F   Petitions for rehearing are frequently granted.

5. T F   The procedure for execution differs, depending upon whether the judgment debtor is an individual or a corporation.

6. T F   The appellant may in some instances pay the costs for appeal.

7. T F   Appellate courts may impose requirements for the format of briefs but not their length.

8. T F   Internal Operating Procedures supplement the Federal Rules of Civil Procedure.

9. T F   Sheriffs cannot execute on a judgment against an individual unless the judgment debtor has filed a schedule of exempt property.

10. T F   The party in whose favor judgment is entered is barred from filing post-verdict motions.

11. T F   A judgment with insufficient Findings of Facts may be overturned on appeal.

12. T F   Interlocutory orders can never be appealed until after the court's final decision is entered.

13. T F   The civil docket is generally indexed both by names of plaintiffs and names of defendants.

14. T F   Once a case has been appealed, the trial court no longer has jurisdiction over it.

15. T F   A judge may set aside a verdict whenever she disagrees with the jury's verdict.

Chapter 13   Post-Trial Procedures and Appeals

ANSWERS TO STUDY QUESTIONS

1. The judge must consider the evidence in the light most favorable to the nonmoving party. If there is insufficient evidence to support the jury's verdict, the judge may grant the motion JNOV. The judge may not properly grant a motion JNOV just because the judge disagrees with the jury's verdict.

2. FRCivP 59 does not enumerate specific grounds. Rather, it states that a new trial may be granted for reasons that courts have used before to grant new trials. Thus the attorney/paralegal team must research the grounds on which motions for new trial have been granted in the jurisdiction previously.

3. A harmless error is one that does not affect the substantial rights of the parties. A trial judge may make errors that, when considered with the totality of everything that happened at trial, did not affect the parties' substantial rights. If the error was not serious, it is not a valid ground for appeal.

4. A judgment is the court's final decision that resolves all matters in dispute between the parties. An interlocutory order is an order entered before the final judgment and applies to only one aspect of the trial, such as the admission of certain evidence or the denial of a jury trial. Interlocutory orders cannot be appealed except in narrow circumstances when the trial judge certifies that immediate appeal is necessary. When final judgment is entered, then all alleged errors at trial can be appealed. This is the final decision rule.

5. Sometimes the judge or the judge's law clerk drafts the judgment. At other times the judge directs the attorneys to submit a judgment. In this instance, the attorney for the prevailing party prepares a draft and lets the other attorney review it. The judgment is then given to the judge for review and signature.

6. First is an introductory paragraph stating the judge presiding and the session of court during which the trial was held. Next come the Findings of Fact, in which the court states the pertinent facts that were found to be true. The next section contains the Conclusions of Law, the judge's conclusions on the legal issues that form the basis of the plaintiff's complaint. This is where the court recites the essential elements of the claims that the prevailing party proved or failed to prove. The judgment concludes with a statement of the relief to which the parties are entitled and a statement as to which party pays the costs.

7. A judgment becomes effective when it is signed by the judge, filed with the clerk of court, and entered in the civil docket by the clerk of court.

8. The bill of costs is a form that the prevailing party completes, delineating the court costs. Sometimes the clerk of court imposes standard fees; otherwise, the costs are expected to be reasonable.

9. One method is attachment, where the sheriff seizes personal property and keeps it until after the judgment is entered. A method to prevent the transfer of real property is to file a notice of lis pendens, a simple statement that the property is the subject of litigation. The notice of lis pendens is entered in the civil docket and gives warning to potential buyers.

10. It is a judgment for which relief is granted automatically when the judgment is entered. An example is a divorce judgment. Obviously it is not necessary to execute on property to make a simple divorce judgment effective.

11. If a federal statute is applicable, the procedures it sets forth are followed. More often there is no applicable federal statute, and the established procedures for execution in the state where the district court sits are used.

12. Individual judgment debtors have the right to assert that certain property is exempt from execution. State constitutions and statutes protect a certain amount of property from execution. The judgment debtor is served with a statement of the judgment entered against him or her and a notice of the right to declare exemptions, together with a schedule to list the allegedly exempt property. If the judgment debtor fails to file a schedule of exempt property within the allotted time, the final writ of execution may issue and the sheriff can proceed with execution. If the judgment debtor does file exemptions, then a hearing is held, usually with a magistrate, to determine what property is actually exempt. Corporations are not given the opportunity to claim exempt property.

13. If a judgment debtor does not have sufficient insurance coverage to pay a judgment, the judgment creditor may receive payment from the proceeds of execution on the judgment debtor's property. However, the judgment debtor may own no property at all or only exempt property. Then you have a judgment-proof debtor. You may go through all the time and expense of litigation only to find out that the judgment entered in your favor cannot be paid.

14. An appeal is not worthwhile in every case. If the judgment entered against the potential appellant is small, then the attorney's fees alone would be more than the judgment entered. Not every case has reversible errors to justify a new trial. A client should not pursue an appeal when there is no chance of winning.

15. The court may enter many interlocutory orders during the trial, covering areas such as the admission of certain evidence. It is the most efficient use of trial and appellate courts to join all alleged errors from the trial into one appeal. An interlocutory order can be immediately appealed only when the trial judge certifies that an immediate appeal is needed.

16. Appellate courts do not retry cases. Rather, they review the record of the proceedings from which you are appealing to determine whether reversible errors were committed. Appellate courts rely on the record on appeal and do not hear new testimony.

17. The Federal Rules of Appellate Procedure, supplemented by internal operating procedures of the Fourth Circuit, which may impose additional procedures such as filing a docket statement.

18. The notice of appeal is filed with the clerk of court of the trial court. It simply states that the appellant is appealing the judgment to the appropriate appellate court. The notice of appeal must be filed within 30 days of entry of the judgment that is the subject of appeal, except that the United States government appellant is allowed 60 days.

19. The clerk of the trial court sends a copy of the notice to the clerk of the appellate court, who enters the appeal on the docket.

20. Yes, FRAP 10 requires the appellant to order the transcript from the court reporter within 10 days of filing the notice of appeal. The court reporter has 30 days to complete the transcript and file it with the clerk of the appellate court. However, an extension may be requested by the court reporter.

21. Paralegals perform basically the same tasks as in trial briefs—preparing drafts of statements of facts, conducting legal research, checking case citations, shepardizing cases, and proofreading.

22. In addition to imposing deadlines for filing the briefs, appellate rules impose requirements for the format and sometimes the content of briefs. The rules may also impose limitations on the length of the briefs.

23. First, the appellant files a brief explaining why reversible error was committed and the appellant should get a new trial. The appellee files a brief in response. The appellant is permitted to file a reply brief to respond to the appellee's contentions.

24. Oral argument is generally limited to 30 minutes at the most. Therefore the attorneys must concentrate on their most convincing points.

ANSWERS TO TEST YOUR KNOWLEDGE

MULTIPLE CHOICE

1. c	6. d
2. e	7. d
3. a	8. c
4. b	9. b
5. d	10. c

TRUE/FALSE

1. T	6. T	11. T
2. T	7. F	12. F
3. T	8. T	13. T
4. F	9. F	14. T
5. T	10. F	15. F